Essential
Japan

by Christopher Knowles

Above: *Kato Jinja Shrine, Kumamoto Castle*

AAA Publishing
1000 AAA Drive, Heathrow, Florida 32746

Above: *warriors are key figures in Japanese mythology*

Front cover: *Eight Hells Spring, Beppu; tunnel of* torii *gates, Tsuwano; girl in kimono*
Back cover: *Tsukiji Fish Market, Tokyo*

Written by Christopher Knowles

Edited, designed and produced by AA Publishing
© Automobile Association Developments Limited 2002
Maps © Automobile Association Developments Limited 1999
Reprinted 2004

The contents of this publication are believed correct at the time of printing. Nevertheless, the publishers cannot accept responsibility for errors or omissions or for changes in details given. We are always grateful to readers who let us know of any errors or omissions they come across, and future printings will be updated accordingly.

Library of Congress Catalog Card Number: on file

ISBN 1-56251-524-1

Published in the United States by AAA Publishing, 1000 AAA Drive, Heathrow, Florida 32746
Published in the United Kingdom By AA Publishing

A02006

Color separation: Pace Colour, Southampton, UK

Printed and bound in Italy by Printer Trento S.r.l.

Find out more about AAA Publishing and the wide range of services the AAA provides by visiting our website at www.aaa.com

Contents

About this Book 4

About this Book

Essential *Japan* is divided into five sections to cover the most important aspects of your visit to Japan.

Viewing Japan pages 5–14
An introduction to Japan by the author.
Japan's Features
Essence of Japan
The Shaping of Japan
Peace and Quiet
Japan's Famous

Top Ten pages 15–26
The author's choice of the Top Ten places to see in Japan, listed in alphabetical order, each with practical information.

What to See pages 27–90
The five main areas of Japan, each with its own brief introduction and an alphabetical listing of the main attractions.
Practical information
Snippets of 'Did you know…' information
4 suggested walks
4 suggested tours
2 features

Where To... pages 91–116
Detailed listings of the best places to eat, stay, shop, take the children and be entertained.

Practical Matters pages 117–24
A highly visual section containing essential travel information.

Maps
All map references are to the individual maps found in the What to See section of this guide.
For example, Fuji-san has the reference ➕ 29C3 – indicating the page on which the map is located and the grid square in which the mountain is to be found. A list of the maps that have been used in this travel guide can be found in the index.

Prices
Where appropriate, an indication of the cost of an establishment is given by **£** signs:
£££ denotes higher prices, **££** denotes average prices, while **£** denotes lower charges.

Star Ratings
Most of the places described in this book have been given a separate rating:

✪✪✪ Do not miss
✪✪ Highly recommended
✪ Worth seeing

Viewing
Japan

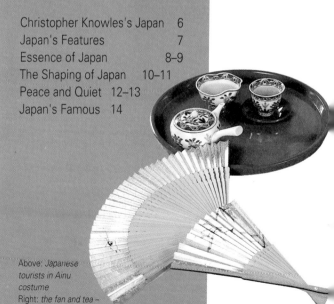

Above: Japanese
tourists in Ainu
costume
Right: the fan and tea –
potent symbols of Japan

Christopher Knowles's Japan

Volcanic Land
Perhaps the Japanese obsession with stability stems from the country's physical instability. A young country geologically, it is peppered with active volcanoes, which provide the universally loved hot springs (*onsen*), and earth tremors occur somewhere almost daily.

Woman in traditional dress, Naha; the Japanese like to maintain strong links with the past

Japan still has that element of mystery about it – rather surprisingly for one of the most thoroughly modern countries in the world. A little bit of Japan, after all, in the form of electronic technology, or of a car, is in almost every home in the developed world.

There are perhaps two principal reasons for this special quality. Firstly, Japan's seclusion from the outside world between 1600 and 1867 fostered an inward-looking mentality that has not made the country's culture readily accessible; and secondly, Japan has yet to become a major tourist destination since it is still thought of as being too expensive and too 'difficult'.

Japan need not be inaccessible. Getting there, it is true, will not be cheap, but once in the country a bit of planning can keep costs at a reasonable level; and although not being able to speak Japanese is a disadvantage, local people do make considerable efforts to be helpful.

As a holiday destination Japan has some distinct advantages – it is well organised, clean and, above all, very safe, as honesty is generally highly valued. At the same time there is still that element of 'exclusion' about Japan, which makes it an exciting country to explore.

Japan's Features

Geography

The total land area of Japan is 377, 435sq km, about 80 per cent of which is mountainous. It is an island nation, a curving archipelago 3,000km in length, consisting of about a thousand islands, which, until some 10,000 years ago, were attached to continental Asia. There are four major islands – Honshu (the largest) in the middle, Hokkaido in the north and Kyushu and Shikoku in the south. Japan's latitude stretches from about 25 degrees in the south to 45 degrees in the north.

The Climate

Because of the length of the country north to south, there are great variations in the climate. Hokkaido is like Siberia – it has short, hot summers and long, cold winters. The Ryuku Islands are sub-tropical with mild winters and hot summers. In the rest of Japan, the summer lasts from June to August and is hot and humid, being especially wet during July, whilst winters are wet and cold, with heavy snow in the western part of Honshu. Elsewhere, temperatures rarely drop below freezing.

The People

Japan is densely populated with 126 million people, of whom about 75 per cent live in cities and towns. It is a country of remarkable ethnic homogeneity, immigration by foreigners being practically unknown. There is really only one people racially distinct from the Japanese – the Ainu, the indigenous people of Hokkaido, of whom about 25,000 still remain. There are also a number of Koreans, who have been rather uneasily assimilated into Japanese life.

Japanese Names

Japanese etiquette is demanding, but as a foreigner you will not be expected to have mastered it. Traditionally family or surnames precede given or forenames, and this is the system followed in this book, except for people universally known in the West by Western convention (such as Kazuo Ishiguro). It is customary to address people by their surname, followed by the honorific 'san'. In some cases the prefix 'o' is used, or both 'o' and 'san' together.

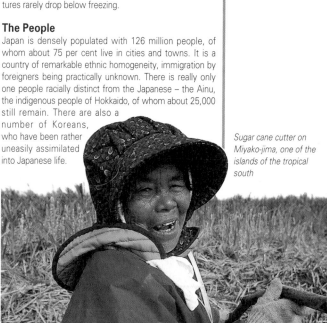

Sugar cane cutter on Miyako-jima, one of the islands of the tropical south

Essence of Japan

Below: the kimono bestows a graceful deportment
Bottom: the bullet train, or Shinkansen, offers comfortable but expensive high-speed travel

The essence of Japan might conveniently be divided into two aspects. There is the ultra-modern urban Japan of big cities that have developed into conurbations, one city melting into another; and there is the Japan of tranquillity, of temples, gardens and shrines, mountains, coast-lines and national parks. Vast areas of the country are only thinly populated, and offer every-thing for the seeker of spiritual contemplation. Contemporary Japan is likely to make the greatest immediate impact on the first-time visitor, however, for all the major cities are essentially modern. Tokyo, in particular, is an immense showground for new architecture and the latest in technology and gadgetry.

THE 10 ESSENTIALS

If you want to get under the skin of the country and of the Japanese, here are some essentials:

• **Visit a *pachinko* parlour.** Every town has its *pachinko* parlours, huge entertainment rooms with row after row of vertical pinball machines patronised by people of all ages.

• **Stay in a *ryokan*.** These are traditional inns, often family run, where the rooms are enclosed with wood and paper walls, where there are *tatami* mats on the floor and where you sleep on a *futon*. They are pricey, but the price will usually include traditional Japanese dinner and breakfast, served in your room.

• **Travel on the bullet train**, or Shinkansen, the express train network that links the major cities. These trains are fast and comfortable, but quite expensive.

• **Eat noisy noodles.** *Ramen*, or Chinese noodles, are Japan's own fast food. Small street establishments sell them hot in a broth to passers-by. Eating them noisily is supposed to enhance the flavour.

• **See *sumo* or *kabuki*,** both quintessential Japanese entertainments. The first is stylised wrestling involving huge fighters (two at a time) trying to push each other over or out of a circle drawn on the floor; the second is a form of theatre in which expansive gestures tell popular folk tales.

• **Visit a public bath.** The Japanese take cleanliness very seriously, but having a traditional bath is also a great pleasure. Soaping takes place separately, so that when you enter the communal hot bath you are already clean.

• **Stay in a capsule hotel.** Not for the claustrophobic, these hotels are space-savers in crowded cities. They feature tiny rooms (2m x 1m x 1m) with bed, TV and radio, lights and alarm clock.

• **Picnic under cherry blossom** in the spring. It used to be traditional to welcome the new season by mounting a small expedition to see the blossom, and this is still a charming way to spend a warm day.

• **See a *geisha* on her way to work.** Although much less conspicuous in recent years, the *geisha* still has a role to play. At dusk in Kyoto and Tokyo *geishas* are still to be seen in full regalia on their way to their first appointments.

Below: *carefully pruned bonsai cherry tree*
Middle: sumo *wrestling*

• **Go to a karaoke**. This is not everybody's idea of a good time except in Japan, where it has become a national institution and can be found all over the country.

Right: *Ginza by night: Tokyo's most famous district is a playground for wealthy businessmen*

The Shaping of Japan

10,000–300 BC
The Jomon period. First signs of Japanese civilisation by peoples probably crossing land bridges from Siberia, Korea and China.

300 BC–AD 300
The Yayoi period. People probably of Chinese or Korean origin develop wet-rice cultivation and use of bronze and iron.

AD 300–710
The Yamato kingdom assumes national leadership and Buddhism takes root.

710
The first permanent Japanese capital is established in Nara. This is modelled on the Chinese capital of Ch'ang-an (Xian).

794–1185
During the Heian period the capital is moved to Heian (Kyoto), where it remains until 1868. Although the frontiers are extended to northern Honshu, the balance of power lies with rival clans.

858
The Fujiwara clan achieves ascendancy at the Heian court, forcing eight successive emperors to step down in favour of easily manipulated children.

1185–1333
The Kamakura period marks the beginning of the rise of the *samurai*. In 1185 the Minamoto family establishes a rival power base in Kamakura, but is defeated by Emperor Go-Daigo.

1274
The first wave of Mongol raiders arrive in Japan and are driven back by typhoons. Seven years later a second attack is defeated in the same way. The Japanese call these storms *kamikaze*, or 'divine winds'.

1333–1573
The Muromachi period. Two rival empires are established, so civil war is a regular feature of this time.

1392
The reunification of the northern and southern courts ensures maintenance of an unbroken imperial line.

1543
Christianity takes root briefly with the arrival of the Portuguese.

1573–1600
The short Momoyama period brings peace and unity under Oda Nobunaga. In 1582 he is betrayed by one of his generals and commits ritual suicide. he eis

succeeded by Toyotomi Hideyoshi.

1590
Reunification completed under Hideyoshi.

1600–1867
The Edo period begins with the defeat of Hideyoshi by Tokugawa Ieyasu, who establishes a capital at Edo (Tokyo). A strict order of rank begins. Japan is closed to the outside world for more than 250 years.

1600
William Adams, the English sailor who is the inspiration for William Clavell's novel *Shogun*, arrives in Japan.

1853
Commodore Perry of the US Navy arrives. His demands for free trade hastens the decline of the corrupt shogunate.

1867–1912
In 1867 the Meiji emperor takes control and abolishes the shogunate. A Western-style constitution is established in 1889, and a resurgent Japan defeats the Chinese in 1894–5 and the Russians in 1904–5.

1910
Korea is annexed as part of Japan's drive for imperial expansion.

The siege of Osaka Castle by Tokugawa in 1615

1926
Emperor Hirohito ascends to the throne.

1931
Expansionist policies combined with a pan-Asian, anti-American stance lead to the invasion of China.

1941
Japan enters World War II with the attack on Pearl Harbour, Hawaii.

1945
Unconditional surrender follows the dropping of atomic bombs on Hiroshima and Nagasaki by the US. A new constitution diminishes the role of the emperor. Japan recovers to become the world's most successful post-war economy.

1990s
The 1990s show some stagnation, with government scandals, the effects of the 1995 Kobe earthquake, and the collapse in 1998 of several major banks.

Since 2000
Although the economy appears to have stabilised, Japan's strict social order has yet to recover its confidence.

Peace & Quiet

National Parks
Japan is richly endowed with national parks. As well as those covered here, some of the most spectacular are described more fully elsewhere:
Akan National Park (▶ 34)
Aso-Kuju National Park (▶ 89)
Iriomote-jima (▶ 19)
Shikotsu-Toya National Park (▶ 39)
Towada-Hachimantai National Park (▶ 39)

The contemplative life is still an integral part of Japanese culture, despite the congested nature of modern living. The population is concentrated in the cities, leaving wide, open spaces aplenty elsewhere, often preserved as national parks. These extensive areas, criss-crossed by quiet roads, can be easily accessed by car, bus and train. Parks and reserves give you the last chance of spying Japan's more unusual fauna, including the Japanese macaque, or 'snow monkey', which bathes in the hot springs of Beppu (▶ 84). The Japanese giant salamander and the Iriomote cat (found in the Ryuku Islands) are both unique to this country. Bears are also indigenous, with brown bears found on Hokkaido, and Asiatic brown bears on Honshu, Kyushu and Shikoku.

Joshin'etsu-kogen National Park
Northwest of Tokyo, and reachable from Ueno Station by train in two hours to Karawizawa, this national park is an area of white birch and Japanese larch woodland on mountain slopes. There are also hot springs, and nature trails leading from the town into the hills.

Odaito, Hokkaido
Located on the east coast of Hokkaido, Odaito is sheltered from the sea by a long sandspit. The dramatic coastal scenery comes to life in winter, when sea eagles swoop between the waves and whooper swans return from their European breeding grounds. In summer the mudflats are home to many other species of wildfowl.

Arasaki Crane Reserve, Kyushu
Located in the southwestern part of the island, this reserve is probably the best place in the country to view the bird most often associated with Japan, the crane. Cranes migrate here in winter from their breeding grounds in continental Asia, attracted by large expanses of rice paddy. The most common species is the hooded crane, but you will see white-necked cranes and perhaps other species such as common, demoiselle and Siberian white

Cranes are revered in Oriental art and mythology for their grace and fidelity; this Japanese (or red-crowned) crane is found on Hokkaido

cranes. Cranes frequently appear in Japanese and Chinese culture as symbols of longevity.

Bandai Kogen and Mount Bandai

This national park is located in Honshu close to Fukushima. Formed as a result of the eruption of Mount Bandai in 1888, in which new lakes were created amid a new landscape, it has wonderful scenery and excellent walking trails. One of the best of these runs around a group of lakes called the Goshikinuma (Five Coloured Lakes).

Daisetsuzan National Park

Japan's largest national park lies at the centre of Hokkaido. An unspoilt area of volcanoes rising to 2,133m, with forest, rivers, gorges and ice fields, it is an excellent place for walkers and lovers of hot spring baths. It lies about 15km east of Kamikawa, which is the gateway to Sounkyo, well known for its hot springs and gorge. West of Sounkyo, the hot spring resort of Asahidake Onsen lies at the foot of Mount Asahidake and can be reached by bus from Asahikawa.

Shiretoko Peninsula

The Shiretoko Peninsula and its national park form an unspoilt volcanic wilderness on the northeast on Hokkaido. Bathe in the warm waters of the Kamuiwakka Falls and enjoy the wonderful views, or try one of the excellent hikes up Mount Rausu-dake or Mount Io. You are advised to take heed of the warnings about bears in this area.

Sacred Mountains, Monasteries and Gardens

Traditionally Japanese gods live on remote mountain tops (for example, Mount Omine on the Kii Peninsula, one of Japan's holiest sites) so visiting their shrines usually requires an arduous journey. Yet pilgrimage is an important ritual in Japan, requiring believers to adopt the appropriate robes, bells and staff. Sometimes monasteries on the holy mountain tops accommodate pilgrims and visitors.

Waterfall in Daisetsuzan, Hokkaido, one of Japan's most unspoiled national parks

Japanese gardens traditionally fall into three categories: the hill garden, where nature is recreated in miniature; the tea garden, a site for the tea ceremony; and the austere Zen 'flat' garden, incorporating rocks and raked gravel, designed as an object of contemplation rather than a representation. Many of the most famous Zen gardens, including that at the Nanzenji Temple, are in Kyoto.

Japan's Famous

Lafcadio Hearn
Perhaps the best-known foreign writer in Japan, Hearn was born in Greece in 1850 of Greco-Irish parents. His early years were spent in Britain and the US, where he worked as a journalist. In 1890 he came to Japan, teaching first at Matsue. He remained in Japan for the rest of his life, adapting Japanese ghost stories and writing about the Japan of the period. He died in 1904.

Renowned author Kazuo Ishiguro has played a key role in boosting Western interest in Japan

Tokugawa Ieyasu

Born in 1542, Tokugawa Ieyasu established the Edo kingdom, which effectively closed Japan to the outside world, between 1600 and 1853. Although he grew up in an era of uncertainty and civil war he managed to become the largest landowner in the country, and by a series of treacherous acts succeeded in seizing supreme power following the Battle of Sekigahara in 1600, when he defeated the heir of the previous ruler, Toyotomi Hideyoshi. He claimed imperial descent and declared himself *shogun* (military leader), with his new capital in Edo (Tokyo). In 1605 he resigned to ensure the longevity of the new dynasty, and he died in 1616. He had reunited Japan by sheer politicking and ruthlessness, and his successors were able to emulate him only by closing Japan's borders, thereby preventing any contamination from the outside world from seeping in.

Kurosawa Akira

One of the founding fathers of Japanese cinema, film director Kurosawa Akira was born in Tokyo in 1910. His work came to international prominence at the 1951 Venice Film Festival, when *Rashomon* won the grand prize. His 1954 film *Shichinin-no-Samurai* (*The Seven Samurai*) was later used as the basis for the epic Western movie *The Magnificent Seven*. His literary adaptations include *Ran* (1985, an interpretation of *King Lear*), and he continued to direct films across a range of genres into old age. He died in 1998.

Kazuo Ishiguro

This British novelist of Japanese extraction was born in Nagasaki in 1954 and came to Britain in 1960. His first novel, written in English, was *A Pale View of Hills*, published in 1982. The narrator is a Japanese widow living in England who has to come to terms with the suicide of her daughter. Her life in Nagasaki at the end of World War II is recalled throughout the book. Ishiguro's subsequent books (after his first two novels) have dealt rather less with Japan, and he is probably now best known for *The Remains of the Day* which was made into a film starring Anthony Hopkins.

Top Ten

Above: *the great Buddha at Kamakura*
Right: *child in school uniform*

1
Fuji-san
(Mount Fuji)

 29C3

 100km southwest of Tokyo

Kawaguchiko (from Hamamatsucho or Shinjuku bus terminals in Tokyo)

Kawaguchiko ☎ (0555) 72 6700; information line in English ☎ (0555) 23 3000 . Closed Sat, Sun, holidays, 28 Dec–3 Jan

The pleasing shape and permanently snow-capped cone of Japan's highest mountain have become an enduring image of the country.

Mount Fuji is in fact a 3,776m-high dormant volcano, which last erupted in 1707. Views of the mountain have been immortalised over the years by Hokusai (1760–1849) and other artists, although modern images of the mountain usually involve a bullet train, blossom and a clear blue sky. In fact, whilst the mountain is certainly visible from the train as it passes close to the town of Fuji, you will be lucky to see its summit uncluttered by mist or cloud.

Walking to the summit of Fuji is possible at any time of year, although the inexperienced should only consider it in the fine weather of July and August. The mountain, which is an object of veneration and pilgrimage for the Japanese, can become crowded. Start from one of the four 'Fifth Stations' (served by bus from various points), of which the highest is Kawaguchiko, leaving a 5–7 hour hike to the top. Anyone of average fitness can undertake this, but bear in mind that the weather is dangerously changeable, and altitude sickness is possible even at these comparatively modest heights.

Unless you are committed to the ascent you are better advised to admire from afar and visit the lakes to the north. From Kawaguchiko, for example, there is a cable-car to the Fuji Viewing Platform and good views are possible from Lake Sai (Sai-ko). The most famous view of Fuji is from Hakone, to the south.

The almost perfectly symmetrical cone of Mount Fuji is best seen from Fuji-Hakone-Izu National Park, looking across Lake Ashi

2
Hagi

This charming old town is an unexpected delight on the peaceful northern shoreline of southwestern Honshu.

 64A2

 90km west of Hiroshima

 Higashi-Hagi

 Hagi on JR San-in line

 Emukai Section
☎ (0838) 25 1750

This comparatively small town was an important centre of the 19th-century movement to restore the emperor to power. One of the leaders of the campaign, Shoin Yoshida, came from Hagi. He was executed in 1859, but his supporters led a revolt that precipitated the final defeat of the *shogun* in 1868.

Most of Hagi is an island surrounded by sea and river. One of the highlights is the old *samurai* residential area in the quarters of Jokamachi, Horiuchi and Teremachi, with whitewashed walls, fascinating houses and temples. Among them is the Kikuya House, built in 1604 for a wealthy merchant whose influence allowed him the rare privilege of living among the *samurai*. The nearby Ishii Chawan Museum is devoted to teaware.

The Kumaya Bijutsukan in the Jokomachi quarter is an art museum housed in small 18th-century warehouses in the gardens of the house of the Kumaya family. The collection includes traditional screens and teaware. Hagi is well known for its pinkish stoneware pottery – there are a number of kilns and shops in the western part of the town.

To the east of the Matsumotogawa River is the Tokoji Temple, with a spectacular lantern-lined path leading to tombs of the Mori clan. The 500 stone lanterns were erected by the lords' servants, and are lit every year on 15 August in a guard of honour.

Top: *traditional* samurai *house*
Above: *the regiments of stone lanterns that lead to the Mori clan's tombs at* Tokoji

17

3
Hiroshima

Hiroshima will always be known as the target of the world's first atomic bomb, but a new city – busy and prosperous – has emerged from the ruins.

Colourful messages and paper cranes left at the Children's Peace Memorial

✚ 64A2

✉ 300km west of Osaka

🚌 Hiroshima

🚆 Hiroshima (Shinkansen and JR Sanyo line) to Tokyo, Kyoto, Hakata and Miyajima

ℹ JR Hiroshima Station
☎ (082) 261 1877

Until the morning of 6 August 1945, Hiroshima had largely escaped the bombing that levelled many other cities in Japan. But then the uranium bomb was dropped from the American aircraft *Enola Gay* at 8:15AM and instantly killed some 75,000 people; the death toll has since risen to nearer 200,000, with people dying from the after-effects of radiation.

The city's heart was completely flattened in the blast, so it will be no surprise to discover that Hiroshima is a thoroughly modern city. The principal items of interest commemorate the events of that day, which, it is thought, continue even now to cause abnormally high levels of cancer among the local people.

The main symbol of the bomb's destruction is the A-Bomb Dome (Gembaku Domu), formerly the Industrial Promotion Hall and now a UNESCO World Heritage Site. The ruin, on the riverbank near Aioi-dori, was one of the few constructions to survive the blast. It is an eerie, moving sight, its church-like tower crowned with the fragile remains of the roof, and there are always piles of paper origami cranes in front of it – the crane symbolising longevity and wisdom.

Just across the river is the Peace Memorial Park (Heiwa-koen), with a cenotaph and a Peace Flame, which will be extinguished at the moment when the last atomic bomb is destroyed. Within the park is the Peace Memorial Museum, a collection of items – watches found after the blast, for example, with the hands frozen at 8:15 – which, in the simplest and starkest way, illustrate this most appalling of all intrusions into the banality of everyday life. In the same area is the Children's Peace Memorial, a statue recalling a young leukaemia victim who was convinced that she would recover if she could fold a thousand paper cranes. She managed 664 before she died. Children now fold paper cranes in her memory..

4
Iriomote-jima

This jungle-covered tropical island in the far south of the Japanese archipelago is a complete contrast to the more temperate north.

If you want to sample a taste of the tropics, then this island is probably your best bet in Japan. It's an area of beaches, forest, rivers and waterfalls, almost four-fifths of the island being national park. It can only be reached by ferry from neighbouring Ishigaki Island, which arrives at the tiny town of Funaura.

For those who don't want to do much more than enjoy the climate, then Iriomote-jima offers some fine beaches, particularly at Haemita-no-hama and Hoshisuna-no-hama. You can also dive from here, in search of the manta rays that abound in these warm waters.

For many the main attraction is a trip along the Urauchi-gawa river to see the Mariudo Falls, set amid lush, glistening vegetation which includes the twisting, sinuous roots of the sakshimasuo trees. After the boat journey there is a walk of just over an hour to the falls and, beyond them, the Kampira Falls, which are elongated into a series of rapids. The walk, on a path through dense jungle, is not difficult, although brushes with vegetation may produce leeches, which are easily despatched with salt or a lighted match. The heat can be intense, but there are good places for swimming near by.

Other excellent walks on the island include the trek from Funaura to the Binai Falls, which offers wonderful views to the sea.

82A1

Fly from Funaura to Ishigaki-jima

Regular service from Ishigaki to Funaura Docks

Canoes and kayaks for hire

A Shinto shrine for fishermen on Iriomote-jima

5

Kamakura

✝ 50C2

✉ 50km south of Tokyo

🕐 Most temples open daily. Kamakura Museum closed Mon

🚌 JR Hase station for the Great Buddha

🚃 Kamakura and Kita-Kamakura (from Shimbashi, Shinagawa and Tokyo stations in Tokyo) to Matsuyama and Beppu

ℹ️ Outside Kamakura station ☎ (0467) 223 350

✋ Entry to temples is generally cheap

A delightful day trip south from Tokyo will take you to one of the most historically important sites in the country – a medieval capital and the home of many beautiful temples and shrines.

In 1192, after years of fighting, power in Japan lay in the hands of the Minamoto clan. When Minamoto Yoritomo became *shogun* he moved the capital from Kyoto to his base in Kamakura. It remained the capital until 1333.

The most famous site in Kamakura is the Great Buddha (Kamakura Daibutsu) to the west of the town, completed in 1252. The Buddha (the Amitabha Buddha, or the Buddha of Salvation) sits in the open air, the hall that housed it destroyed by a tidal wave in the 15th century. Made of bronze, it weighs over 800 tons and is 11.4m high. It is considered an artistic masterpiece.

The Tsuruguaka Hachiman-gu Shrine, in the north of the town, is dedicated to Hachiman, guardian of the Minamoto clan and also the god of war. Close to the entrance is the Kamakura Museum, displaying early ceramics and teaware in vibrant and unusual designs.

The Engakuji Temple is one of the principal Rinzai Zen temples in Kamakura and has pleasant gardens and a number of smaller temples, of which the most interesting is the Shari-den, or the Shrine of the Sacred Tooth of Buddha. The Engakuji Bell is the largest in the town.

The most important temple of Kamakura, as well as the most picturesque, is the attractive Kenchoji Temple, located to the north of the town and founded in 1253 as a seminary for Zen monks. Although the remaining buildings are mostly reconstructions, the Zen gardens are charming and there are plenty of quiet paths to follow in the surrounding woods.

Among the many other temples and shrines in and around Kamakura, others worth visiting are the Zeniarai Benten, reached through a stone tunnel cut into a steep rock face, where you can wash coins to guarantee prosperity; the active Hokokuji with its pretty gardens; and the Sugimoto-dera, thought to be the oldest temple in the town, founded in AD 734.

Although most of the important sites of Kamakura can be visited in a day, on foot and by bus, a two-day visit would be both more restful and more rewarding.

Above: *classical Japanese temple architecture at the Kenchoji temple*
Opposite: *the great Buddha is a miracle of artistic engineering*

6
Kanazawa

50A3

150km north of Nagoya

Services to Kyoto, Nagoya and Tokyo

JR limited express to Kyoto, Nagoya and Osaka

Frequent flights to all main cities: airport 55mins from city centre

Kanazawa station
(076) 232 6200

Kenrokuen Garden embodies all that is best in a Japanese garden

Kanazawa is a large, modern city that yet retains many reminders of the old Japan, which kept faith with the idea of the unity of heaven and earth.

Located on the western coast of central Honshu, in Ishikawa-ken, Kanazawa became an independent Buddhist republic during the 15th century, before being taken over by the Maeda clan. It is still a religious centre, as well as a centre for crafts and the arts, particularly *noh* (stylised dance drama) theatre.

The single most famous attraction of Kanazawa, and one of Japan's three finest gardens, is the Kenrokuen Garden. Originally part of the castle, the private domain of the Maeda, the garden was gradually enlarged between the 16th and 19th centuries. It lives up to its name, which refers to the six vital features of a garden – artifice, age, running water, seclusion, spaciousness and views – and is best seen in the peace of early morning.

But what is most attractive about Kanazawa is the abundance of old houses, especially in the *samurai* quarter

behind the 109 Korinbo department store in the Nagamachi district. The Nomura Family House, the elegant former home of a wealthy *samurai* warrior, has been painstakingly maintained in its original condition and is open to the public.

The Higashi-yama district overlooks the city from the slopes of Utatsuyama Mountain. There are a number of temples and shrines throughout the district, some active, some decaying, whilst the Eastern Pleasure Quarter, just north of the Asano-gawa river, was established as an entertainment area for high-ranking citizens in 1820. There are several streets of old *geisha* houses, one of which, the Shima-ke, is open to the public.

Also worth seeing is the Honda Museum with its family collection of armour and art, the intimate Gyokusenen Garden and the Ohi Pottery Museum.

7
Kinkakuji Temple, Kyoto

One of Japan's best-known sights, the Temple of the Golden Pavilion is resplendent in its beautiful garden setting.

Kyoto has so many temples and gardens that it is perhaps invidious to single out any particular ones among them; but there are one or two that have achieved, for various reasons, particular fame, and Kinkakuji, or the Golden Pavilion, is chief among these.

Located in the northwest of the city, it was originally built in 1397 as a country retirement villa for Yoshimitsu, the third Ashikaga *shogun*, whose son later converted it to a temple. It has clearly exerted a grip on the Japanese ever since; so much so that it was burned to the ground in 1950 by a monk obsessed with its gilded charm.

Reconstruction of the pavilion began in 1955. Covered in gold leaf five times the original thickness, the reborn pavilion was completed only in 1987. Although to the layman it is an exquisite example of classical Japanese architecture, the pavilion is actually in three styles. The first floor is 'palace' style, representing the Heian period, the apogee of courtly elegance; the second is '*samurai* house' style, like a temple hall, with a statue of Kannon Bosatsu; and the third is austere, bare 'Zen temple' style, with a statue of Amida, the Buddha of the Pure Land.

The Golden Pavilion – the most beautiful among a number of pavilions on the site – sits on the edge of a lake dotted with islets and surrounded by woodland, which, on still days, perfectly mirrors it in its waters.

✚ 64C2

✉ Kinkakuji-michi, Kyoto

🕐 Daily 9–5

🚌 59, 205

♿ None

✋ Cheap

The Golden Pavilion – vulgar extravagance or idyllic beauty?

8
Miyajima

<table>
<tr><td>✚</td><td>64A2</td></tr>
<tr><td>✉</td><td>15km south of Hiroshima</td></tr>
<tr><td>🕐</td><td>Itsukushima Shrine: daily 6:30 to sunset</td></tr>
<tr><td>🚆</td><td>Hiroshima to Miyajima-guchi (25mins)</td></tr>
<tr><td>⛴</td><td>Regular service from Hiroshima Ujina port and from mainland ferry terminal at Miyajima-guchi. Information from ferry building ☎ (0829) 944 2011</td></tr>
<tr><td>✋</td><td>Cheap</td></tr>
</table>

Miyajima (Shrine Island), just off the coast of Honshu, is famous for its many holy sites, above all Itsukushima Shrine with its 'floating' torii gate.

Miyajima, easily reachable from Hiroshima, was originally named after its famous Itsukushima Shinto shrine, which dates back to the 6th century. Now the entire island has been dedicated as a shrine and is considered one of Japan's 'three famous views'.

Since the island was considered holy, ordinary mortals were not permitted to set foot on it, but had to visit the shrine by boat, entering through the floating wooden *torii* gate in the bay. The present-day version was built in 1875 in traditional Japanese style, painted red and rooted in the mudflats; it is best seen at high tide, when it seems to float above the water. It looks especially spectacular at night if the lamps in the gate gallery are lit.

To the north of the shrine is the Senjokaku Hall. Built in 1587, it is a massive timber construction decorated with paintings, and conveys a wonderful atmosphere of grandeur. Its name means 'Pavilion of 1,000 Mats'.

Elsewhere on the island there are a number of other temples, museums and walks to enjoy. The Miyajima Museum of History and Folklore is in a 19th-century

The 'floating' torii, the sacred entrance to the Itsukushima Shrine on Miyajima

merchant's house, with a charming garden, whilst the Daisho-in Temple, to the south of the town, is an interesting jumble of pavilions, gardens and pools.

The walk up Mount Misen (530m) in the centre of the island is worth undertaking for its views. Cable-cars can take you a large part of the way, leaving just a short stroll to the summit.

9
Todaiji Temple, Nara

The main attraction of the historic town of Nara is this temple, which houses a giant bronze Buddha in the largest wooden building in the world.

The sheer magnitude of the gargantuan bronze Buddha (weighing in at 437 tons and over 16m high) is alone worth the visit to Nara. The statue is a masterpiece that took five years to cast, and crippled the economy in the process of its creation.

The main hall is called the Daibutsuden (Hall of the Great Buddha); as you approach it you will pass a pair of 13th-century carved wooden guardians by the Nandaimon gate, considered to be among the finest in Japan. The current incarnation of the hall is of comparatively recent construction, built in 1709, and is two-thirds the size of preceding halls; but the Buddha within was first made in AD 746 to the orders of Emperor Shomu, as a symbol of his power and perhaps as a charm against a smallpox epidemic that was raging at the time. Earthquakes and other disasters have naturally taken their toll over the centuries, and the current version of the statue dates from the Edo period.

Just north of the Daibutsuden hall is the Shosoin (Treasure Repository); this wooden building used to hold the imperial treasures, but these are now exhibited twice a year in the Nara National Museum.

The Kasuga Taisha Shrine, set in the deer-filled grounds, is adorned with scores of lanterns, which are a feature of the twice-yearly lantern festivals held here.

64C2

Nara-koen Park, Nara

Nov–Feb 8–4:30; Mar 8–5; Apr–Sep 7:30–5:30; Oct 7:30–5

1, 2

Nara City Tourist Centre, near station ☎ (0742) 22 3900

Cheap

Above: *the magnificent wooden hall that houses the Great Buddha is, at 48m high, itself an impressive feat of engineering*

25

10
Tsukiji Fish Market, Tokyo

✠ 45E1

✉ Tsukiji, Tokyo

🕐 Mon–Sat 3–10. Closed holidays and Aug 15–16

🚉 Tsukiji (Honganji Temple exit)

✋ Free

Seen at its best in the early morning, the lively Tsukiji Fish Market offers a fascinating insight into the daily life of this fish-loving nation.

Located in the Tsukiji District in the southern part of the city, Tokyo Fish Market is the largest in Japan and probably the world. It swings into action at about 3AM, just as the first fishing boats start arriving – not only from around the Japanese coast but also from Africa and the Americas – to deliver their catches. The larger fish, like the precious tuna, are numbered, and by 5AM an auction for wholesalers (not open to the public) is under way.

Finally, purchases are transferred to stalls in the market for sale to restaurants and retailers. The enormous covered market handles just about all the fish consumed in Tokyo – it is a vast area, busy with fishmongers hacking and slicing at every sea creature imaginable (and some unimaginable).

Next to the market are rows of *sushi* restaurants, whilst between the market and the Tsukiji metro station seafood stalls and shops linked to the fish trade abound. If you manage to arrive by 7:30AM, you will find that the market is still in full swing. Waterproof footwear is highly recommended.

Fresh fish and seafood are key ingredients of Japanese cooking

What to See

Above: *Lake Ashi, in Fuji-Hakone-Izu National Park*
Right: *statue of Kobo Daishi, founder of Zentsuji Temple, Takamatsu*

See Tokyo from the
water: tour boats on the
Sumida River, Asakusa

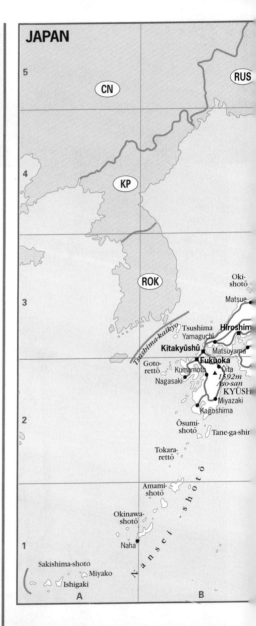

JAPAN

5

CN

RUS

4

KP

ROK

3

Oki-
shotō

Matsue

Tsushima-kaikyō

Tsushima   Hiroshim

Yamaguchi

Kitakyūshū

Matsuyama

Goto-
rettō   Kumamoto   Fukuoka

Ōita

Nagasaki

1592m
Aso-san   KYŪSH

Miyazaki

Kagoshima

Ōsumi-
shotō   Tane-ga-shir

Tokara-
rettō

Nansei-shotō

2

Amami-
shotō

Okinawa-
shotō

Naha

1

Sakishima-shotō

Miyako

Ishigaki

A

B

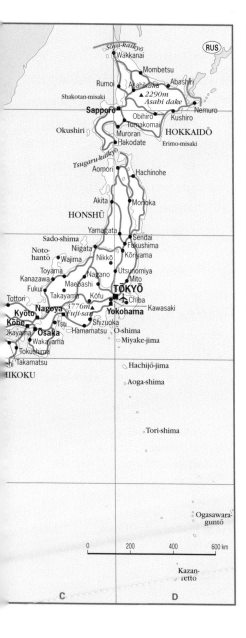

A small fast food fan in Fukuoka

Hokkaido &
Northern Honshu

This region of Japan combines Hokkaido, the northernmost island of the Japanese archipelago and the second largest, with the northern part (Tohoku province) of its neighbour, the largest and principal island of Honshu. Both areas have a rural, rugged terrain and majestic scenery, and are comparatively untouched by tourism. There are also some big differences, however – Hokkaido has a Siberian climate, for example, whilst northern Honshu is generally more temperate.

Tohoku is essentially mountainous and the best area to see something of unspoilt, rural Japan and its folk traditions. Hokkaido, which is home to only 5 per cent of the Japanese population, is especially renowned for its scenery, wildlife and outdoor pursuits. It is also the last remaining outpost of the Ainu, the original inhabitants of Japan, who are racially akin to the people of Siberia.

> *' The Countrey of Japan is very large and spacious … it is Mountainous and craggie, full of Rockes and stonie places '*

ARTHUR HATCH,
A Letter Touching Japan (1623), in
Purchas his Pilgrimes (1625)

Sapporo

With a population of approaching 2 million, Sapporo is the administrative seat of Hokkaido and its main population centre. It is also a prosperous city and the primary focus of cultural life on the island.

Although essentially a brand-new city, with comparatively little in the way of sights for the tourist, Sapporo is lively and cosmopolitan, with nightlife possibilities as exciting as anywhere in Japan. It is a very pleasant place to stay for a couple of days or to use as a base for visits elsewhere on the island. The absence of crowds, futhermore, and its less frantic way of life make Sapporo a comfortable window on modern Japan.

Sapporo's history is tied in with the history of Hokkaido. Although a colony was established here in the 16th century, until the Meiji Restoration, Hokkaido (or Ezo as it was called) was all but an irrelevance to the rulers of Japan – an inhospitable place occupied by a barbarous indigenous people, the Ainu. After 1868 the government encouraged people from elsewhere in Japan to settle here and foreign experts were employed to advise on agriculture. Sapporo began to expand from this time, its basic layout the work of an American architect.

Sapporo offers some of the best nightlife in Japan

 33B4

View along Odori Park and across Sapporo from the TV Tower

What to See in Sapporo

BOTANICAL GARDEN AND BATCHELOR MUSEUM ★

Run by the Faculty of Agriculture of Hokkaido University, the Botanical Garden covers about 14 hectares and is planted with areas of virgin forest and about 5,000 varieties of flora native to Hokkaido.

In the grounds of the garden is the former house of an English anthropologist, John Batchelor, which now houses a small museum devoted to the Ainu, with examples of traditional clothing, tools and other items unique to the indigenous people of Hokkaido. The Ainu have no written language, but a rich oral tradition of folk poems.

ODORI PARK ★

This green thoroughfare stretches through the city centre. At one end is the TV Tower with a 90m observation platform. The park is also the site of the annual Ice Festival held every February since 1950, which is famous for its intricate snow sculptures.

SAPPORO BEER GARDEN AND MUSEUM ★★

'Sapporo' is one of the best Japanese beers, and the first brewery in Japan was established here in 1876. On the site of the original brewery there is now a museum and a beer hall that serves beer and hearty foods. The speciality is 'Ghengis-Khan Barbecue', a sort of Mongolian hotpot, and there are also 'all you can eat for a set price' deals.

TOKEIDAI CLOCK TOWER ★

Built in 1878 in Russian style, the clock tower, beside the City Hall, is the symbol of the city and a notable landmark, so is usually surrounded by crowds of Japanese tourists. It houses a small museum of local history.

☒ Hokkaido University
🕐 29 Apr–30 Sep 9–4; 1 Oct–3 Nov 9–3:30. Closed Mon. Between 4 Nov and 28 Apr only the greenhouse is open 10–3. Closed Sun and holidays
🚇 Sapporo 11 chome Subway station
🖐 Cheap

☒ Odori-koen
🕐 TV Tower daily summer, 9:20–8, winter, 10–6
🚇 Odori
🖐 TV Tower: moderate

☒ 1.5km east of station
🕐 Daily. Brewery tours May–Sep 9–3:40 (Jun–Aug 9–4:40). Beer garden daily 11:30–9
🚇 Higashi-Kuyakusho-mae
🖐 Free

☒ 0.5km south of Sapporo train station
🕐 Museum Tue–Sun, 9:30–4:30

Traditional beer-lovers from an old advertisement in the
Sapporo Beer Museum

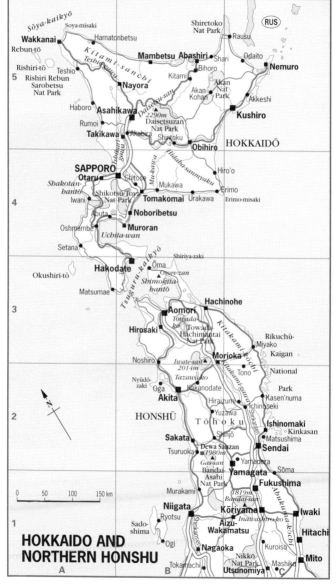

HOKKAIDO AND NORTHERN HONSHU

What to See in Hokkaido & Northern Honshu

AKAN NATIONAL PARK ⊕⊕

The park covers a large area of forest, volcanoes and lakes (905sq km) in the eastern part of Hokkaido. The main centres are Akan Kohan on Lake Akan; Kawayu Onsen, a hot-spring resort convenient for visiting Lake Kussharo, Hokkaido's largest lake; and Mount Io, with its clouds of steam and excellent walking trail. Lake Mashu is famous for its clear water and is best seen from its western side. There are hiking trails to follow at various locations – maps are available from tourist information centres.

🔲 33B5
✉ 300km northeast of Sapporo
⊙ Daily
🚌 Akan Kohan Bus Centre
🚉 Kawayu from Bihoro (north) or Kushiro (south)
ℹ Akan Kohan Visitor Centre ☎ (0154) 67 3200
💷 Free

Autumn in Hokkaido: the limpid waters of Lake Akan

Did you know ?

Until the Meiji Restoration, Hokkaido was not formally part of Japan. Apart from one clan area, it was open to Russian occupation, a fact that hastened its incorporation into the new state.

HAKODATE ⊕⊕

Located on the coast towards the south of Hokkaido, Hakodate, the island's original capital, was one of the first ports open to foreigners in 1854. Russians, in particular, settled here and some of their houses remain, in the Motomachi quarter. The old walls of the Goryokaku Fortress, now set in a park, was built in Western style as a defence against the Russians. From Mount Hakodate, reached by cable-car, there are terrific views across the town.

🔲 33B3
✉ 150km southwest of Sapporo
🚌 Hakodate Harbour View Hotel for buses to Sapporo
ℹ Hakodate Station, ☎ (0138) 235 440

Around Hakodate

Set off from the Hakodate Station and proceed west along the waterfront street.

A Sunday morning market operates near the station.

Pass the Old Hakodate post office on your right, and continue past the Kanemori Warehouses.

A number of interesting cafés and shops have sprung up in this old corner of the town, and are well worth exploring.

Bear right to head north, following the coastline. After about three quarters of a kilometre turn left, and cross the tram lines to reach the Chinese Memorial Hall. Turn left after this, heading into the Motomachi District to pass the green onion domes of the Russian Orthodox Church.

The Motomachi District was an area inhabited largely by foreigners, and the Orthodox Church, built in 1862, stands out among several Western-style buildings.

Continue to the Sanroku Station, and take a tram to the summit of Mount Hakodate.

This is one of Japan's celebrated 'three great views', and not to be missed. It's especially dramatic at night.

Return east from the tram station, crossing the tramlines. Walk back along the waterfront to Hakodate Railway Station.

Distance
About 4.5km

Time
About 2 hours plus stops

Start/End point
Hakodate Station
✚ 33B3

Lunch
There are cafés and restaurants in Kanemori, and a café on the summit of Mount Hakodate

Trams, old and new, are still an integral part of daily life in Hakodate

🚩 33C2
✉ 100km north of Sendai
🚌 Regular buses from
Ichinoseki to Hiraizumi to
Chusonji Temple
🚆 Tohoku Shinkansen to
Ichinoseki and then bus;
or JR to Hiraizumi
ℹ Hiraizumi Station
☎ (0191) 462 111

HIRAIZUMI ★★

The small town of Hiraizumi lies on the eastern part of northern Honshu, and is accessible by short train or bus rides from Ichinoseki; throughout the 12th century, it was a clan town to rival Kyoto, its prosperity founded on gold mines owned by the Fujiwara clan. Their finest legacy is the Chusonji Temple, where the Golden Hall, in lacquer, gold leaf and mother of pearl, is a marvel. The Motsuji Temple is ruined, but has a fine garden that is still used for dance and flower festivals.

🚩 33B3
✉ 250km north of Sendai
🚌 Services to Morioka and
Lake Towadako
🚆 Direct links to Aomori and
Akita
ℹ Hirosaki Station
☎ (0172) 320 524

Above: *the dramatic
mountain backdrop to the
lush greenery around
Kakunodate*

HIROSAKI ★★

Hirosaki was the political centre of the northwestern part of Honshu until the Meiji Restoration. Outside its modern centre it has managed to retain much of its charm – there are some old *samurai* houses in the north of the town, close to the Neputa-mura Museum, which is laid out as a historic village. The Saisho-in Temple has a lovely 17th-century pagoda; of the other temples the most impressive is undoubtedly the Choshoji, with its 17th-century hall and Tsugaru clan mausoleum. The town has a thriving tradition of craftwork – look out for the local speciality, Tsugaru-nuri, a tough lacquerware renowned for it durability.

🚩 33B2
✉ 150km northwest of Sendai
🚌 Regular buses to Akita
and Tazawako
🚆 Direct links to Akita,
Morioka, Tazawako
ℹ Kakunodate Station
☎ (0187) 54 2700

KAKUNODATE ★★

This small town in northern Honshu is worth visiting for its splendid collection of original *samurai* houses. Look out for the Kawarada-ke House, and the neighbouring Samurai Shiryokan, a *samurai* museum. The Denshokan Museum is dedicated to ceramics, armour and cherry-bark carving, whilst the Hirafuku Memorial Art Museum shows crafts from around the region.

Not quite the real thing, but a waxwork samurai at Matsushima

MATSUSHIMA ★★

Matsushima lies on the east coast of Honshu just north of Sendai. Worth seeing in the town are the Kanran-tei Pavilion and especially the Zuiganji Temple, one of the finest in the region. The real highlight, however, is the bay, with its many pine-clad islands: this is one of the 'three great views' of Japan and is especially beautiful at sunset. Cruises depart regularly from the harbour.

33C2

✉ 30km northeast of Sendai

🚆 Senseki line from Sendai to Matsushima-Kaigan or Shiogama

🚢 Ferry from Shiogama

ℹ Matsushima-Kaigan Station ☎ (022) 354 2263

OTARU ★

A port on the western coast of Hokkaido, Otaru is chiefly noted for its architecture, dating back to the late 19th/early 20th centuries when the port played a significant role in the development of the island. The most interesting buildings are to be found in the harbour area and along the Otaru Canal, which is prettily lined with lamps. The architecture reflects both Western and Japanese styles, and two buildings really stand out – the old Mitsui Bank and the former Nippon Yusen Company. The town museum is located in an old traditional warehouse dating from 1893.

33A4

✉ 30km west of Sapporo

🚌 Frequent buses to Sapporo

🚆 Train from Sapporo on JR Hakodate line

ℹ Otaru Station ☎ (0134) 291 333

SADO-SHIMA ★★

Lying off the northwest coast of Honshu, this mountainous island was once a place of exile, but is now an oasis of rural tranquillity. Visit Aikawa, with its fascinating gold mine and folk museum; Mano, the medieval capital; and Sawata, for the Myoshoji Temple set in the hills.

33B1

✉ 40km off west coast of Honshu

🚢 Regular ferry and hydrofoil services between Ryotsu and Niigata, Naoetsu and Ogi

✈ Regular flights between Ryotsu and Niigata

ℹ Niigata Kotsu Information Centre, Ryotsu ☎ (0259) 23 3300

Enjoy a ride in one of the traditional wash-tub boats of Sado Island

Otaru Cycle Ride

Distance
Maximum of 150km

Time
2 days

Start/End point
Otaru
33A4

Lunch
Nikka distillery

For bike hire ☎ (0134) 331 661

This is a scenic coastal ride of about 150km around part of the Shakotan-hanto Peninsula. It can be done in two ways – cycle for half a day and then back again, or cycle as far as Irika or Hizuka, where there is accommodation. Check out cycle hire at the tourist information centre, or bring a bike by ferry from Niigata or Tsuraga.

Take the coastal Route 5 westwards out of Otaru and cycle to Yoichi.

Pause at the Nikka distillery en route, which specialises in whiskey and apple wine, and also serves local dishes.

Continue along the coast on Route 229 to Furubira. Continue through Furubira and carry on towards Shakotan.

Keep left to stay on the 229 as it goes inland before rejoining the coast at Nozuka, where there is a good beach.

Turn right here to follow the coast.

Pass through villages that make a living from fishing and seaweed, and close to the lighthouse at the Shakotan-misaki Cape.

The road loops around and eventually rejoins the 229 which you can follow back to Otaru.

SENDAI ✪

The largest city of Tohoku is Sendai. Although you may find a short stay here useful for transport connections, or for exploring the traditional rural life of neighbouring Yamagata prefecture, it is not a major tourist centre. Aobajo Castle was built in 1602 by Date Masamune, one of the most powerful feudal lords in late 16th- and early 17th-century Japan, who made Sendai his base; the castle was destroyed by bombing in World War II. A computerised film shows how the castle would have once looked.

> ✚ 33C2
> ✉ 290km north of Tokyo
> 🚌 Direct buses from Tokyo (8 hours)
> 🚆 Thoku Shinkansen from Tokyo (2 hours)
> ✈ Regular flights to Okinawa, Osaka, Sapporo
> ℹ Sendai Station ☎ (022) 222 3269

SHIKOTSU-TOYA NATIONAL PARK ✪✪✪

Within easy reach of Sapporo, this park of almost 1,000sq km, centred around the two lakes of Shikotsu and Toya, offers a superb combination of splendid scenery (take a cruise on Lake Shikotsu to enoy the views), numerous hiking trails, volcanoes and hot springs. The popular hot spring spa of Noboribetsu Onsen in the south of the park is well worth exploring, especially the dramatic volcanic crater of Jigokudani (Hell Valley) to the north of the resort, where the constant wisps of steam rise eerily from the pools of boiling water created by volcanic activity.

> ✚ 33B4
> ✉ Just south of Sapporo
> 🚌 From Sapporo to Lake Shikotsu
> 🚆 Toya or Noboribetsu Stations on JR Hakodate line, then bus
> ℹ Near bus terminal at Lake Shikotsu ☎ (0123) 25 2404

TOWADA-HACHIMANTAI NATIONAL PARK ✪

This park in northern central Tohoku is renowned for its hot springs (especially Sukayu Onsen with its 1,000-person bath), the beautiful scenery around Towada Lake (a volcanic crater) and the volcanic landscape of the Hachimantai Plateau, where there are more thermal resorts, including Goshogake Onsen and Toshichi Onsen. There are excellent walking possibilities in the hills around the lake (the main entry point being Yasumiya), especially at Oirase-keiryu.

> ✚ 33B3
> ✉ 250km north of Sendai
> 🚌 From Aomori, Morioka or Hirosaki to Towadako and from Towadako to Hachimantai
> 🚆 Towada Minami on JR Hanawa Line
> ℹ National Park ☎ (0176) 75 2506

Jigokudani, Shikotsu-Toya National Park: specially constructed walkways allow close-up views of the steaming pools and encrusted mineral formations that have given the valley its name

Central Honshu

The region of Central Honshu includes Tokyo, the capital of Japan and its largest city, with its surroundings; and the area known as Chubu,  which stretches across Honshu with Tokyo and Kyoto its northern and southern points.

Of course the region is dominated by the sheer size and influence of Tokyo, which is sure to figure on any itinerary in Japan. There is much more, however – Mount Fuji falls within this area, as do the major cities of Nikko and Yokohama. There is the wonderful scenery of Noto-hanto (Noto Peninsula) to be enjoyed, and Nagano, the charming town of Takayama, the splendid castle of Inuyama and the artistic and cultural treasures of Kanazawa. If you go nowhere else in Japan, this region will provide a good insight into the nature of the country.

'*Immense silences – green and romantic – alternate with quarters of turmoil and factories and railroad stations.*'

LAFCADIO HEARN (on Tokyo),
Letter to Ellwood Hendrick (1897)

————————•————————

Giant ornamental lantern at the Asakusa Kannon Temple, Tokyo's best-loved temple

The throng along Nakamise-dori, the intriguing shopping street leading to the Kannon Temple

Japanese beauty at a festival in Asakusa

Tokyo

The Japanese capital, with a population of some 12 million, is a vast, seemingly endless metropolis, merging seamlessly with neighbouring towns. It has no real centre, but a number of neighbourhoods, each with its own character.

Tokyo was little more than a village by the name of Edo until 1603, when it became the seat of the Tokugawa shogunate. Kyoto, the then capital, was marginalised as a result, allowing Edo to grow substantially during the period of Japanese isolation (the Edo period) until the Meiji Restoration. The new Emperor Meiji adopted Edo as his capital in 1868 and renamed it 'Eastern Capital', or Tokyo. Modernisation became the watchword then, a theme that has continued to this day – and indeed it is 'modernity' that is one of the most interesting characteristics of Tokyo today.

What can you do in Tokyo? Everything. There are a few historic sights that have survived earthquakes and warfare, and plenty of museums; but the main thing is to experience the city itself, with its fabulous shops and restaurants, its nightlife, its fascinating fish market, the highlife in Shinjuku and Ginza, and lowlife in Kabukicho and Roppongi.

The comprehensive metro system, in conjunction with local trains, provides the best way of getting around town.

What to See in Tokyo (by Area)

AKIHABARA ⊙⊙

This area of Tokyo is a must for anyone interested in buying electronic goods. Electronic Town sells anything and everything (including items which may never make it on to the general market) through 600 shops and stores.

✚ 45E4
🕐 Some shops open until 9PM

> ### Did you know ?
>
> *A typical Japanese address is preceded by numbers, for example 1–2–3. '1' refers to the smallest administrative town section, a 'chome'. The '2' refers to perhaps a block within the chome. The '3' refers to a single building.*

ASAKUSA ⊙⊙⊙

An area in the northeast of the city with a distinctive character, Asakusa is the old downtown or *shitamachi* quarter. It is home to the oldest and best known temple in Tokyo, the Sensoji (or **Asakusa Kannon Temple**), which has been standing here – in various forms – since AD 628. Nakamise-dori, in front of it, consists of several fascinating rows of gaudy shops and stalls selling snack foods, traditional gifts and souvenirs. Asakusa was the old pleasure area and *geishas* can still be spotted in the evenings. Boat cruises along the Sumida-gawa river begin and end at the Azuma Bridge.

✚ 45F5

Asakusa Kannon Temple
✉ 2-3-1 Asakusa, Taito-ku
🕐 Daily 6AM–sunset
None
Free

GINZA ⊙⊙⊙

The one part of Tokyo that everyone knows is the richest part of the city, a mixture, in London terms, of Mayfair and Knightsbridge. There is plenty of 'quality' but it also holds plenty of snob appeal – it is an area of expensive boutiques, department stores and exclusive galleries. The central point is Ginza 4-chome Crossing. Of interest is the Yoseido Gallery, which specialises in the sale of modern

✚ 45D2
🕐 Shops and stores 10–6.
Wako closed Sun.
Nihonsu closed Thu.
Yoseido closed Sun

Japanese prints at 5-5-15 Ginza; the International Arcade selling tax-free items at the railway end of Miyuki Dori; the Sony Building at 5-3-1 Ginza with its restaurants and boutiques; the Wako Department Store, topped by the famous Hattori Clock Tower, on Ginza 4-chome Crossing; and the Nihonsu Centre at 5-9-1 Ginza, where you can taste *sake*.

Above: *Shinto prayer boards at Asakusa Kannon Temple*
Left: sumo *wrestlers are not an unusual sight on Tokyo's streets*

43

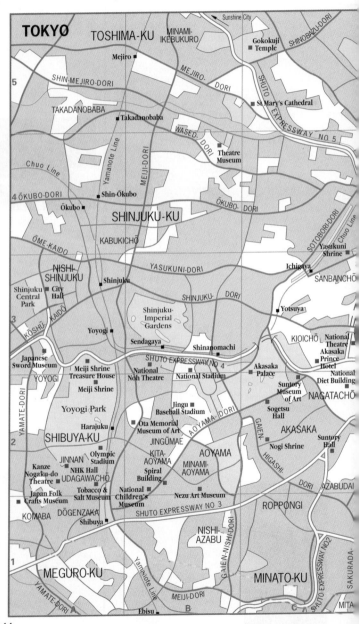

TOKYO

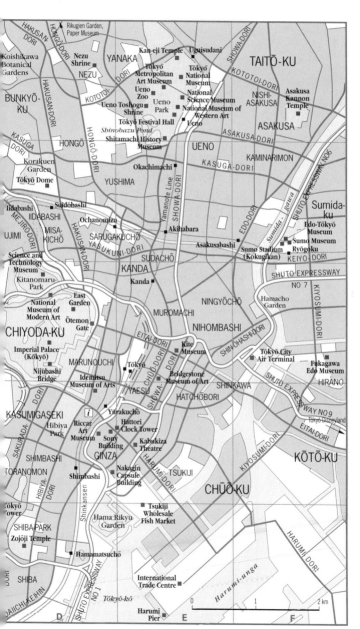

44A2

Nezu Fine Art Museum
- 6-5-36 Minami Aoyama, Minato-ku
- (03) 3400 2536
- 9:30–4:30. Closed Mon and 15 Dec–5 Jan
- Few
- Expensive

Meiji Shrine (Meiji-jingu)
- 1-1 Kamizono-cho, Yoyogi, Shibuya-ku
- Sunrise–sunset
- Free

The Meiji Shrine, dedicated to the spirit of Emperor Meiji and his wife, Empress Shoken, was built by voluntary labour in 1920

45D3

National Museum of Modern Art
- Kintamaru Koen Park
- (03) 3214 2561
- Tue–Thu, Sat–Sun 10–5, Fri 10–8
- Few
- Moderate

Yasukuni Shrine
44C3
- 3-1-1 Kudankita, Chiyuda-ku
- Sunrise–sunset
- Free

HARAJUKU ⭐⭐

The centre for the teenage fashion scene, until recently Harajuku was well known to tourists for the Sunday displays of amateur talent in Yoyogi-koen Park and on Omotesando-dori close to the Olympic Stadium. Several hundred young people, many dressed in 1950s rock'n'roll regalia once congregated here, performing to the appropriate music. This is now prohibited, but the area is still a centre for youth culture. The **Nezu Fine Art Museum** is worth seeing for painting, tea ceremony demonstrations and beautiful gardens, and don't miss the attractive and historic **Meiji Shrine**.

HIBIYA AND IMPERIAL PALACE AREA ⭐⭐

Hibiya is largely taken up with the Imperial Palace (Kokyo), the home of the Japanese Imperial Family, which dominates the centre of Tokyo. The current building dates from 1968, replacing the original of 1888, and its forerunner, Edo Castle. The palace is open only twice a year – 2 January and 23 December – but the East Garden is open five days a week and views of the palace are possible from near the Nijubashi Bridge. The **National Museum of Modern Art** is worth visiting, and look out for the **Yasukuni Shrine**, dedicated to Japan's war dead since 1853; since many of these died in imperialistic wars, the shrine has been at the centre of political controversies.

Did you know ?

If you walk around the entertainment areas of major cities, you are sure to notice gaudy, kitsch buildings in the form of castles and other fantasies. These are 'Love Hotels' where rooms are rented by the hour to lovers in search of privacy. In many the rooms have themes to suit the moods of the customers.

IKEBUKURO ✪

Located in the northwest of the city, and off the tourist route, Ikebukuro is interesting for some high-tech displays (the Toyota Amlux building, with a 'smellorama' cinema and everything to do with the auto world), two of the largest department stores in the world (Tobu, closed Wednesday, and Seibu, closed Thursday) and the Metropolitan Art Space, designed specifically for performance art. The 17th-century **Rikugien Garden**, a 10-hectare Edo pleasure garden of gravel paths and pine trees, is close to JR Komagome Station.

ROPPONGI ✪✪

By day visitors are drawn here by the 330m Tokyo Tower , with its two observation platforms and Holographic Mystery Zone; and the nearby Zojoji Temple which dates back to 1605. As night falls, however, the place is transformed into a compendium of bars and clubs, open to all hours, and featuring Japanese versions of Western hip, for this is the nightlife centre of Tokyo.

SHIBUYA ✪✪

Shibuya is another area noted for its shops, department stores (particularly Seibu and Tokyu) and fervent commercialism, aimed mostly at younger people. Spain-dori has a host of shops selling fashion items. Tokyu-Hands, by contrast, is famous for its eight floors of hobby supplies and toys. The **Tokyu Bunkamura** is a huge complex of cinemas, shops, a museum and theatres. Arrive at opening time at any of the department stores to see the employees bow to the first customers of the day.

✚ 44B5

Rikugien Garden

✉ South of JR Komagome Station

🕐 9–2:30. Closed Mon

🖐 Cheap

✚ 44C1

Below: *Nijubashi Bridge and the Imperial Palace*

✚ 44A1

Tokyu Bunkamura

✉ 2-24-1 Dogenzaka

☎ (03) 3477 3111

🕐 Tokyu department store 10–7:30. Closed Tue. Bunkamura daily

Shinjuku Gyoen
+ 44B3
✉ 11 Naitocho, Shinjuku-ku
☎ (03) 3350 0151
🕐 9–4. Closed Mon
🚹 None
🍴 Cheap

SHINJUKU

This area, in the west of the city, now probably best represents modern Tokyo – its railway station complex alone is like a small city, and the district was the inspiration for the film *Bladerunner*. The Shinjuku NS Building houses the largest clock in the world; and one of the buildings that make up the Metropolitan Government Offices was until recently the tallest building in the country. There are bustling underground shopping arcades, and the area west of the station is probably the best in Japan for buying cameras. Northeast of the station is Tokyo's notorious red-light district, Kabukicho, which is an amusing place to stroll around – outrageous, but perfectly safe. **Shinjuku Gyoen** (Shinjuku Imperial Gardens) is an 80-hectare public garden, particularly popular with local residents. The gardens include one in the formal 19th-century French style.

TSUKIJI FISH MARKET (➤ 26, TOP TEN)

+ 45E5

Tokyo National Museum
✉ Ueno Park, Taito-ku
☎ (03) 3822 1111
🕐 9–4. Closed Mon. Only parts of the museum are open at any one time
🍴 Cheap

National Museum of Western Art
✉ Ueno Park, Taito-ku
☎ (03) 3822 1111
🕐 9:30–5. Closed Mon
🍴 Cheap

UENO

Behind the busy railway station area lies Ueno Park, Tokyo's largest park and a popular venue for viewing the cherry blossom in spring. The area is home to several great museums. The vast **Tokyo National Museum** has superb exhibits from every field of Japanese art and archaeology; a special highlight is the Horyuji Gallery with its priceless treasures of religious art. The Tokyo Metropolitan Art Museum exhibits modern Japanese art, while the **National Museum of Western Art** building was designed by Le Corbusier, and its collection is dominated by French masterpieces of the 19th and 20th centuries. The nearby Shitamachi History Museum records the heritage of pre-war Tokyo.

Above: inspirational contemporary architecture in Shinjuku

Exploring Asakusa

Start at Asakusa metro station.

Across the road from the station is the Asakusa TIC. An unusual clock above the entrance springs some wonderful surprises when it strikes the hour. From the metro locate the ornate Kaminarimon Gate, with its lantern and statues of the thunder and rain gods.

Walk through the gate and along Nakamise-dori towards the Sensoji or Kannon Temple.

At the end of the street lined with stalls is the temple itself, the oldest and most revered in Tokyo, dedicated to Kannon, the Buddhist Goddess of Mercy. Here is a counter where you can purchase a long wooden stick with a number on it. The number corresponds to a number on a set of drawers. Inside will be your fortune – translation is available at a nearby counter.

Explore to the left (west) of the temple, for an old area of bars, restaurants, 'love hotels' and music halls. Cross Kokusai-dori and continue straight on, with the tower of the Asakusa View Hotel on your right. Reach Kappabashi-dori.

This is the heart of Tokyo's wholesale catering trade, and you can buy everything from the sharpest kitchen knives to gaudy decorative food made from plastic.

Retrace your steps to return to Asakusa metro station.

Distance
3km

Time
1½ hours

Start/End point
Asakusa Metro Station
✉ 45F5

Lunch
There are many restaurants along the route, especially close to Nakamise-dori

The Asakusa Kannon Temple, where you can find your fortune (and have it translated)

49

Did you know?

The novel Shogun *by James Clavell was based on the life of the English sailor William Adams. After a storm blew his ship to Kyushu his shipbuilding skills were exploited by the shogun, Tokugawa Ieyasu. Adams spent the rest of his life in Edo, Japan, where he died in 1620.*

Sailor Will Adams is commemorated at Ito on the Izu Peninsula

CENTRAL HONSHU

0   50   100 km

What to See in Central Honshu

FUJI-SAN (► 16, TOP TEN)

INUYAMA   ✪✪
Located north of Nagoya, this medium-sized town has several attractions of interest. **Inuyama Castle**, dating from 1440, overlooks the river and is one of the few original medieval castles in Japan. Near by stands the **Uraku-en Garden** and within it the Jo-an Tea House, one of Japan's finest. Inuyama is also a centre for cormorant fishing. The birds 'ukai' are tethered to the boats, with a leash around the neck to prevent them swallowing the fish they catch – usually a delicacy called *ayu*.

KAMIKOCHI   ✪✪
Surrounded by the glorious scenery of the Japan Alps, Kamikochi is a base for outdoor enthusiasts. There are plenty of walks and hikes to suit all levels of competence. Not far away, the Shirahone Onsen is a famous hot spring resort which serves as a base for walks around the Norikura Plateau. You can also enjoy (from June to October) the scenic bus route known around here as the Norikura Skyline Road.

KAMAKURA (► 20–1, TOP TEN)

KANAZAWA (► 23, TOP TEN)

➕ 50A2
✉ 25km north of Nagoya
🚌 Regular service from Nagoya
🚄 Direct from Shin-Nagoya on the Meitetsu Line
ℹ Inuyama Station
   ☎ (0568) 611 800.
   Fishing season Jun–Sep

Inuyama Castle
✉ 0.75km southwest of station
🕐 Daily 9–4:30
♿ None
💰 Cheap

Uraku-en Garden
✉ 0.5km southwest of station
🕐 Daily 9–5; Dec–Feb 9–4
♿ None
💰 Moderate

The splendid walking country around Kamikochi, at the heart of the Japan Alps

---

➕ 50B3
✉ 125km northeast of Nagoya
🚌 From Shin Shimajima, mid-Apr to mid-Nov only
🚄 Shin Shimajima (service from Matsumoto)
ℹ Kamikochi Bus Station
   ☎ (0263) 952405

☩ 50B3
⊠ 120km northeast of
   Nagoya
⬛ Direct services to
   Nagoya, Osaka, Tokyo
   Shinjuku)
🚃 Direct services to
   Nagoya, Tokyo (Shinjuku)
ℹ Matsumoto Station
   ☎ (0263) 322 814

☩ 50B3
⊠ 170km northeast of
   Nagoya
🚃 Direct links to
   Matsumoto, Nagoya and
   Tokyo (Ueno);
   Shinkansen from Tokyo
ℹ Nagano Station
   ☎ (0262) 265 626

Zenkoji Temple
⊠ Motozen-machi
🕐 Daily 5–4; Oct–Apr 6–4
♿ None
👋 Cheap
❓ Gokaicho Festival 10
   Apr–20 May every 7
   years; due 1999

Above: *Matsumoto
Castle, a magnificent
symbol of clan power in
feudal Japan*
Right: *a Buddhist monk in
traditional costume,
Nagano*

MATSUMOTO ★

Popular among hikers who want to explore the Japan Alps, Matsumoto is a modern city set on a high plateau against a dramtic backdrop of snow-capped mountains. Matsumoto Castle, which has original features including a magnificent three-turreted donjon, dates back to 1595 and is one of the best-preserved in Japan. The Nihon Minzoku Shiryokan (Folklore Museum) next door is home to an impressive collection of clocks. There is also a fine museum dedicated to the art of woodblock printing (*ukiyo-e*).

NAGANO ★★

Nagano, host of the 1998 Winter Olympics, is a small town in the midst of beautiful mountain scenery, and is now just under 2 hours from Tokyo by Shinkansen. The town itself is famous for the **Zenkoji Temple**, originally built in the 7th century by Yoshimitsu Honda to house the first Buddhist image in Japan. Hugely popular, it is ecumenical, welcoming people of all Buddhist sects. Pilgrims shuffle into the darkness inside to touch the large, heavy 'key of paradise' to ensure salvation. There is good walking near Nagano at Togakushi, and at Jogokudani Onsen there are famous hot springs. Hakuba, to the north-west, is another excellent walking area, along the old Salt Road, around Nishina Three Lakes and in the Tsugaike Park.

NAGOYA

Rebuilt after World War II, Nagoya is a key industrial centre and home to two of Japan's national treasures. The **Atsuta Jingu Shrine** dates from the 3rd century and is one of the most important in Japan; it houses the sacred sword (not on view to visitors), handed down by the goddess Amaterasu o Mikami. **Nagoya Castle** (rebuilt in 1959) was originally constructed in the 17th century by one of Japan's greatest leaders, Tokugawa Ieyasu, and contains a museum of armour and family heirlooms. The two gilded bronze dolphins on the roof are to protect the castle from fire. The port area is also interesting, with a Maritime Museum and Aquarium.

50A2
120km east of Kyoto
Direct services to Kyoto, Osaka and Tokyo
Direct services to Kyoto, Osaka and Tokyo
Ferry link to Sendai and Hokkaido (Tomakomai)
Direct links to all major cities
Nagoya Station ☎ (052) 541 4301

Atsuta Jingu Shrine
1-1-1 Jingu, Atsuta-ku
24 hours
Meijo subway to Shayakushu station
None
Free

Nagoya Castle
Shiyakusho
Daily 9:30–4:30
Meijo subway to Shayakushu station
Few
Moderate

Elaborate detail on the mausoleum of Tokugawa Ieyasu, founder of the isolationist Edo shogunate

NIKKO

Within striking distance of Tokyo and lying at the centre of over 1,400sq km of spectacular national park, Nikko should be included on any itinerary. Once a seminary for novice monks, it was chosen as the site for the mausoleum of Tokugawa Ieyasu, who established the isolationist Edo shogunate in 1600. The mausoleum (**Toshogu Shrine**), consisting of several pavilions and halls, was actually begun by a grandson of Tokugawa in 1634 and is extraordinary for its venerable aspect and for the level of detail in the decoration that is so uncharacteristic of Japanese art. The famous trio of wise monkeys – 'Hear No Evil, See No Evil, Speak No Evil' – originated here, carved on the lintel of the Sacred Stable for White Horse.

50C3
140km north of Tokyo
Direct service from Tokyo (Asakusa) on Tobu-Nikko line
Kyodo Centre ☎ (0288) 533 795
Toshugu Shrine Grand Festival 17/18 May

Toshogu Shrine
Daily, 8:30–5; Dec–Feb 9–4:30
Expensive

53

From Nikko into Hot-Spring Country

Distance
120km

Time
6 hours

Start/End point
Nikko town
➕ 50C3

Lunch
Nikko Prince Hotel

This drive takes you through Nikko and then along a winding mountain road close to many famous hot springs.

Start from Nikko railway station and head west to the Toshogu Shrine (➤ 53). Continue west along the Irohazaka road (Route 120) towards Lake Chuzenji, passing the Nikko Prince Hotel.

Lake Chuzenji, which reaches a depth of 161m, is known for its setting and vivid blue water. The spectacular 97m Kagon-no-taki (Kagon Waterfall) can be viewed with the lake from the cable-car platform at Chuzenji Onsen.

Head north to join Route 121, which takes you south to the Ryuokyo Valley and Kinugawa Onsen.

Kinugawa Onsen is a famous hot spring, much loved by the Japanese. Nearby Nikko Edo Village is a historic re-creation.

Head back north along Route 121 and then take Route 400 through Shiobara, before branching off towards Toda, Itamuro and Nasugomoto. Continue to Tohokujidoshado, and then join the highway back to Nikko.

Kagon-no-taki waterfall

TAKAYAMA ✪✪

Lying among the Japan Alps, Takayama is famous for its woodcarving and colourful festivals. With a number of unspoilt, traditional streets, particularly in the Sanmachi Suji area, it is a pleasant place to stroll around for a day. Special sights include **Hida Folklore Village**, an open-air museum of traditional thatched farmhouses. Near the river, the Yoshijima Merchant House is distinguished by its elegant decorative detail, while carved images by a wandering 17th-century priest are the highlight of the Takayama Museum of Local History. Two festivals, on 14–15 April and 9–10 October, are well known throughout Japan for sacred music, beautiful floats and above all for puppets, manipulated with astounding skill.

Within striking distance of Takayama is the Shokawa Valley, noted for its traditonal villages.

<table>
<tr><td>✚</td><td>50A3</td></tr>
<tr><td>✉</td><td>120km north of Nagoya</td></tr>
<tr><td>🚌</td><td>Direct links to Kamikochi, Norikura (erratic in winter)</td></tr>
<tr><td>🚆</td><td>Direct service to Nagoya</td></tr>
<tr><td>ℹ</td><td>Hida TIC, Takayama Station ☎ (0577) 325 328</td></tr>
</table>

Hida Folklore Village

<table>
<tr><td>✉</td><td>1-5-90 Kamiokamotocho, Takayama</td></tr>
<tr><td>🕐</td><td>Daily 8:30–5</td></tr>
<tr><td>💰</td><td>Expensive</td></tr>
</table>

YOKOHAMA ✪✪

Japan's second city and premier port is almost physically inseparable from Tokyo, and is popular as a day trip destination. It was one of the first towns to open to foreign trade after the Edo Period (in 1858), and retains its cosmopolitan flavour. Chinatown (*chukagai*), close to the harbour, is especially famous for offering the best Chinese food in the country. In the southeastern part of the city the exquisitely landscaped **Sankei-en Garden** features a 500-year-old pagoda, tea houses and farmhouses. Minato Mirai, by contrast, is a futuristic development with Japan's tallest building, the **Landmark Tower**, which features the world's fastest lift and a viewing platform on the 70th floor; and Cosmo World, home of the world's biggest Ferris wheel.

<table>
<tr><td>✚</td><td>50C2</td></tr>
<tr><td>✉</td><td>20km southwest of Tokyo</td></tr>
<tr><td>🚆</td><td>Regular direct service to Tokyo</td></tr>
<tr><td>ℹ</td><td>Yokohama TIC, Sakragi-cho Station ☎ (045) 211 0111</td></tr>
</table>

Sankei-en Garden

<table>
<tr><td>✉</td><td>Hommuku-Sannotani, Naka-ku</td></tr>
<tr><td>🕐</td><td>Daily, 9–4:30. Closed 29–31 Jan</td></tr>
<tr><td>♿</td><td>None</td></tr>
<tr><td>💰</td><td>Moderate</td></tr>
</table>

Landmark Tower

<table>
<tr><td>✉</td><td>Sakura Dora</td></tr>
<tr><td>☎</td><td>Daily 10–9 (10–10 Sat and daily through Jul/Aug)</td></tr>
<tr><td>🚌</td><td>Blue Line Loop bus</td></tr>
<tr><td>♿</td><td>Few</td></tr>
</table>

The gaudy gateway to Yokohama's Chinatown

Western Honshu & Shikoku

Three areas make up this part of Japan. The first is still known by the vague name of Kansai, meaning 'west of the barrier', referring to the 10th-century frontier with the neighbouring region of Kanto. It encompasses the historical and cultural centres of Nara and Kyoto, as well as the quintessentially modern city of Osaka and the resort area of Wakayama. The rest of mainland Honshu to the west (known as Chugoku) is of greatest interest along its coastlines, with historic Hagi on the rural north coast, and the crowded more urban southern shore, including the tragically famous city of Hiroshima and the scenic area of islands known as the Inland Sea. Shikoku, the third area and the one least known to visitors, boasts magnificent mountain scenery, several of the few remaining original castles in Japan, and the pilgrimage route known as the '88 Temple Circuit'.

> *' At first, the sense of existence here is like that of escaping from an almost unbearable atmospheric pressure into a rarefied, highly oxygenated medium. '*

LAFCADIO HEARN, Letter to Basil Hall Chamberlain (1891)

Kyoto

Japan's former capital is touted as everything that Japan was and everything that foreign visitors want Japan to be. Kyoto can, in parts, measure up to expectations; but it is also a thoroughly modern city.

Anyone coming from Osaka to Kyoto by train – only 15 minutes by Shinkansen – will be surprised to find that the two cities are all but one urban sprawl. The only difference will be the pleasing sight of pagodas and temples breaking the Kyoto skyline. And there are plenty of temples and shrines to explore, at least 2,000 of them, probably too many even for the most avid seeker of spiritual nirvana. Judicious planning is therefore advisable in order to enjoy the highlights and ensure variety.

Kyoto is not only temples and the imperial palace. There are some very intriguing streets to wander and some excellent nightlife to be enjoyed. There are worthwhile museums, a *sake* brewery to visit and interesting excursions possible in the neighbouring countryside.

Much of the city can be explored on foot. Otherwise there is a comprehensive bus service and a single metro line, which is occasionally useful.

Young schoolboys

✚ 64C2

Fan shop in Kyoto; beautifully made, hand-decorated fans can be extremely expensive

What to See in Kyoto

DAITOKUJI ✪✪✪

- Daitokuji-mae, Kita-ku
- Daily 9–4:30
- 205, 206
- None
- Moderate

The arresting simplicity of the Daisen-in Zen garden

The Daitokuji, or Temple of Great Virtue, consists of the main temple plus 23 smaller temples on one extensive site, including ornamental gardens and tea houses. Founded in 1319 and rebuilt during the 15th and 16th centuries after a fire, for many this is the ultimate Zen temple. If you are able only to visit one of the Daitokuji temples, choose Daisen-in, with its handsome Zen garden. Go early to avoid the crowds.

FUSHIMI INARI TAISHA ✪✪✪

- Fukakusa Yabunouchi-cho, Fushima-ku
- Daily sunrise–sunset
- Inari on JR Nara line
- None
- Free
- Festivals on 1 and 8 April

Located in the southern suburbs of Kyoto, and dating back to the 8th century, this is the most important of all the many shrines dedicated to Inari, the god of rice and wealth. Popular with businessmen who come to pray for success and prosperity, the shrine's most distinctive features are the hundreds of red temple gates (*torii*) built over the hillside of Mount Inari, and the shrine temples with their stone foxes, the fox being Inari's earthly representative. A day can easily be spent wandering here.

GINKAKUJI TEMPLE ✪✪✪

- Ginkakuji-mae, Sakyo-ku
- 15 Mar–30 Nov daily 8:30–5; 1 Dec–14 Mar daily 9–4:30
- 5, 203
- Kehan Electric main line to Demachi-yanagi
- None
- Moderate

The Silver Pavilion, in the eastern part of the city, is one of Kyoto's most famous sights. Its name speaks more of intention than of fact – if the *shogun* Yoshimasa had had the funds in 1482, his pleasure villa, later to be converted into a temple, would have been covered in silver. In the event he had to settle for wood. Nonetheless, it is an elegant building, with a raked gravel garden before it, and paths meandering up the wooded hillside behind it.

Kyoto Temples

This is a fairly short stroll along the old canal, which is lined with cherry trees and runs between the Ginkakuji and Nanzenji Temples.

From Ginkakuji-michi bus stop head east and cross the canal to reach the Ginkakuji Temple (► 58). Return to cross the canal and turn immediately left along the alley by the canal.

This is known as the Path of Philosophy and was named after philosopher Nishida Kitaro (1870–1945), who famously compared Western and Zen philosophies.

Continue along the path for just over a kilometre, with the canal on your left.

A short diversion may be made over the canal to see the secluded Honen-in Temple with its traditional raked gardens.

Where the path ends at a road, turn right, passing the Eikando (Zenrinji) Temple on the left.

This temple is set in beautiful gardens with many maple trees. If you have the energy, climb the stairs to the top of the pagoda to enjoy the superb view of Kyoto.

Turn left to pass the Nomura Art Museum on the right.

The museum houses an interesting collection of tea ceremony artefacts.

Continue, bearing right and then left before reaching the Nanzenji Temple.

Now the headquarters of the Rinzai Zen Buddhism, this magnificent temple is reached via the huge Sanmon Gate.

The Nanzenji Temple combines elegance, harmony and tradition

Distance
3km

Time
1 hour

Start/End point
Ginkakuji-michi/Nanzenji Temple
 5, 206

Lunch
Buddhist vegetarian food at entrance to Nanzenji Temple; try the *yudofu* (simmered tofu)

📷 206

❓ Cherry Blossom Dance daily throughout Apr at Gion Kobu Kaburenjo Theatre

A young apprentice geisha, or maiko

GION ✪✪✪

Gion, the former *geisha* district to the east of the Kamo-gawa river, remains one of the most charming areas in Kyoto. There are still plenty of old houses and shops in the area, some dating from the 17th century. Along Hanami-koji in the early evening you can still catch a glimpse of *geisha* or *maiko* girls (often in pairs) shuffling along on their high wooden clogs, or being delivered to their first evening appointments by taxi or limousine. Shinmonzen-dori is lined with antique shops. Gion Corner is a theatre which presents Japanese cultural evenings.

> ### *Did you know ?*
>
> Geisha *girls go through a long apprenticeship before being able to entertain their own clients. They learn to please men mostly through their cultural accomplishments, but their appearance is also important and traditionally they used nightingale droppings as a face cream.*

✉ Kyoto Gyoen-Nai, Kamigyo-ku

☎ (075) 211 1215

🕐 Guided tours Mon–Fri 10 and 2, and at 10 on third Sat of each month except Apr, May, Oct and Nov

🚇 Imadegawa

🚌 59, 203

🎟 Free

GOSHO (IMPERIAL PALACE) ✪✪

The present Imperial Palace was built in 1855, the last of many built on the site since AD 794. Investitures are still held here. It consists of several under-stated palaces linked by corridors and situated in grand gardens in the centre of the city. Tickets have to be reserved in advance for the short guided tour past the main appartments.

✉ Jingumichi, Nishi-Tennocho, Okazaki, Sakyo-ku

🕐 15 Mar–31 Aug 8:30–5:30; 1 Sep–14 Mar 8:30–4:30

🚌 5, 2

🚉 Marutamachi on Keihan line (1km walk)

HEIAN SHRINE ✪✪

Thie Shrine of Peace and Tranquillity in the centre of the city is dedicated to the first and last emperors to reign in Kyoto. It was built in 1895 as a replica of the original Heian period imperial palace in gaudy vermilion and green, and features an enormous *torii* gate. The large garden is famous for its cherry blossom in spring, lotus flowers in summer and maple trees in autumn.

KINKAKUJI TEMPLE (► 23, TOP TEN)

KYOTO NATIONAL MUSEUM ✪✪

Located in the southeastern part of the city in a building that looks as if it had been lifted directly from 19th-century Paris, this museum is housed in two sections and specialises in Buddhist art. The extensive collection is shown in constantly changing displays, and includes neolithic relics from the Jomon and Yayoi periods, ceramics, bronze images, calligraphy, gold screens and burial urns, as well as handicrafts and fine arts.

MOUNT HIEI ✪✪

Overlooking the city to the northeast of Kyoto, Mount Hiei is the splendid site of the Enryakuji Temple. Spread across the summit, and divided into two sections, it was founded in AD 788 for the Tenzai sect of Buddhism. At one stage it boasted 3,000 buildings and several thousand monks, who marked disagreement with imperial policy by descending to the city and destroying rival institutions. Their influence was finally curtailed in 1571, and the temple destroyed. About 100 buildings were rebuilt, including the Kompon Chudo Hall of 1642 in the Todo section and the Shakado Hall in the atmospheric Saito section.

✉ Yamato-oji-dori, Higashiyama-ku
🕐 9–4:30. Closed Mon
🚌 206, 208
💰 Cheap

Below: *the Heian Shrine is a two-thirds scale replica of the first imperial palace*

🕐 Temple: Apr–Nov 8–4:30; Dec–Mar 9–4
🚌 Ohara by Kyoto suburban bus 17, 18 then cable-car; bus stop at Yase-Yeunchi from Kyoto
🚉 Yaseyuan on Eizan line then cable-car and ropeway
💰 Cheap

Nijojo-cho, Nakagyo-ku
Daily 8:45–4. Closed 26 Dec–4 Jan
None
Oike station
9, 50, 51, 67
JR San-in line, Nijo station
None
Moderate

Shijo
12, 203, 207

Kitsuji-dori, 13 Goryoshita-machi, Okyu-ku
Apr–Nov 8–5, Dec–Mar 8:30–4:30
59
JR Hanazono, San-in line
None
Cheap

NIJO CASTLE

Built in 1603 as the residence of the first *shogun*, this ornate and palatial castle was intended to show the emperor that the shogunate was there to stay. The inner and most finely decorated chambers were accessible to none but the highest ranks, though even the outer rooms, beyond which commoners could not pass, were designed to instil awe. The famed 'nightingale floors' were made to creak at the slightest footfall to deter assassins. The Ohiroma Hall, in particular, retains its splendour, as does the Ninomaru Garden.

PONTOCHO

Just to the west of the Kamo-gawa river, roughly opposite Gion, is the traditional centre of Kyoto nightlife. It is really a long, narrow street lined on both sides with bars, restaurants and tea houses, many of which were, and some of which still are, *geisha* establishments and therefore usually out of bounds to foreigners. It is an attractive and faintly mysterious street, an intriguing place for an evening stroll. Parallel with it is Kiyamachi-dori, another lively area of restaurants and bars of a more open nature.

RYOANJI

This temple (the Temple of the Peaceful Dragon) is famous above all for its Zen garden. A perfectly raked expanse (30m by 10m) of gravel with a few painstakingly placed rocks – fifteen in groups of five – it is said to have been created by Soami, a famous ink-line artist who, with a few simple strokes, evokes or suggests a scene. If overcrowding in a garden is thought vulgar, then this minimalist example is the least vulgar of gardens.

What to See in Western Honshu & Shikoku

HAGI (▶ 17, TOP TEN)

HIROSHIMA (▶ 18, TOP TEN)

ISE-SHIMA ✪✪

The Shima Peninsula on the east coast is famous for the Ise Jingu Shrines, the most important Shinto shrines in Japan, devoted to the sun goddess Amaterasu o Mikami, the ancestral divinity of the imperial line. Part of the shrine, which must be rebuilt every 20 years, is surrounded by beautiful cedar woods, and each morning offerings are made in the presence of a white stallion from the imperial stables. Certain areas of the shrine, which is divided into two sections 6km apart, are closed to all but imperial family members. Ise-shima is also well known for its beautiful coastline and beaches and for Mikimoto Island, a pearl cultivation centre.

A priest enjoying the shade at a shrine on Ise-shima

- 🗺 50A1
- ✉ 100km southeast of Osaka
- 🚉 Direct links from Ise to Kyoto, Nagoya, Osaka
- 🚌 Regular bus service between shrines
- ℹ Kashikojima Kintetsu
- ❓ Grand Festival 15–17 Oct

KOBE ✪

Devastated by an earthquake in 1995, Kobe, in an attractive location by the sea and one of the earliest ports to open to the West, has recovered well. Traces of the port's history are evident through the large Chinatown and variety of architectural styles, especially in Kitano-cho. The interesting **Kobe City Museum** is devoted to the history of the town and its relationship with the West.

- 🗺 64C2
- ✉ 50km west of Kyoto
- 🚉 Shinkansen services to Shin-Kobe from Kyoto, Osaka and Tokyo
- 🚢 Naga Pier and Higashi-Kobe for ferries to Awajishima, Kyushu and Shikoku
- ℹ Sannomiya Station
  - ☎ (078) 322 0220
- ❓ Rice Planting Festival 3 Apr to mid-May, Kobe Matsuri

Kobe City Museum
- ✉ 0.75km south of railway station, 24 Kyomachi, Chuo-ku
- ☎ (078) 391 0035
- 🕙 10–5. Closed Mon, 28 Dec–4 Jan
- ♿ Few
- 💴 Cheap

Did you know ?

Many temples and pilgrimages are dedicated to Kannon. Nothing to do with firearms, the name in fact means 'the one who hears the cries of the world' and refers to a bodhisattva, one who vows to achieve enlightenment but who postpones buddhahood to help others and who is the personification of infinite compassion.

Left: *raked gravel and rocks create a peaceful if sterile atmosphere in the Ryoanji Temple garden*

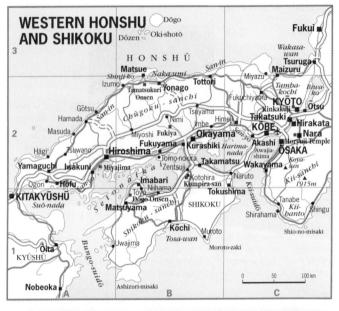

WESTERN HONSHU AND SHIKOKU

KOYA-SAN (MOUNT KOYA)

The first Buddhist monasteries were established on this mountain plateau in AD 816 in a beautiful natural setting, and the symbol of the mountain is the Great Pagoda, found in the Danjogaran temple. In nearby Kongobuji there are wondrous 16th-century painted screens, and the beautiful tree-shaded cemetery is the burial place of many eminent Japanese. For real peace and quiet you may stay in one of the temples and take part in the rituals of monastic Buddhist life.

- 64C2
- Daily 8–5
- Gokurakubashi, then cable-car, then bus
- Senjuinbashi-mae
  ☎ (0736) 562 616
- Moderate
- Aoba Matsuri Festival 15 Jun. Mando Kuyoe Festival 13 Aug

KURASHIKI

The main reason for visiting this pretty town, once prosperous through rice production and textiles, is its old-world picturesqueness. The old quarter, surrounded by the modern town, centres on the canal and Ivy Square, collectively known as Bikan. Here are Edo period houses and warehouses, many of which have become museums. Worth noting in particular is the **Kurashiki Folkcraft Museum**, whose slogan is 'Usability Equals Beauty', and the **Japan Rural Toy Museum**. The Ohara Museum of Art houses the extraordinary collection of European art formerly belonging to the textile baron Ohara Keisaburo (1880–1943). There are paintings by Cézanne, Renoir, El Greco, Degas and many others.

- 64B2
- 20km south of Okayama
- Regular bus service from Okayama
- Kurashiki (local train from Okayama)
- Kurashiki Station
  ☎ (086) 426 8681

Folkcraft Museum
- Bikan, alongside Kurashiki-gawa Canal
- Mar–Nov 9–5; Dec–Feb 9–4:15. Closed Mon
- Moderate

Japan Rural Toy Museum
- Bikan, alongside Kurashiki-gawa Canal
- Daily 9–5
- Few
- Cheap

Left: *a samurai in full fighting regalia*
Opposite: *bright goldfish at a Matsue tea house*

MATSUE

A castle town straddling the Ohashi-gawa river, Matsue was immortalised in the writings of Lafcadio Hearn (➤ 14), who married a local girl and lived here from 1890. The castle (Matsue-jo) is original and dates from 1611. **Lafcadio Hearn's Residence** at the northern end of the old *samurai* street of Shiomi Nawate is much visited by the Japanese, who are intrigued by a foreigner's view of Japan – a museum about his life is next door. Most charming is the Meimei-an Tea House, with its delightful garden and view of the castle.

- 64B3
- 250km west of Kyoto
- Matsue on the JR San-in Line
- Matsue Station
  ☎ (0852) 21 4034

Lafcadio Hearn Residence
- 9–12:30, 1:30–4:30. Closed Wed
- Cheap

MIYAJIMA (➤ 24, TOP TEN)

Food & Drink

Japanese cooking may certainly be counted among the world's great cuisines and is surely one of the healthiest.

Nutritious noodles are available as a snack in most streets

The Japanese Diet

The emphasis tends to be on freshness and simplicity. Expertise is concentrated not only on the cooking but on judicious seasoning, on careful use of the knife and on the final presentation. But the key to Japanese cooking is the freshness of the ingredients. Vegetables tend to be eaten raw, pickled, boiled or steamed; fish (raw or cooked) and rice feature in almost every meal, including breakfast.

Japanese food comes in small but varied parcels. *Sushi* refers to vinegared rice balls with a savoury morsel, often raw fish, on top. *Sashimi* is raw fish served with *wasabi*, a deliciously hot horseradish sauce. *Tempura* is seafood or vegetables dipped in a very light batter and deep-fried in sesame oil. For *sukiyaki*, thinly sliced beef and vegetables are cooked quickly in a hot soy stock and then dipped into raw egg. For *shabu-shabu* the food is dipped into a hot broth and then into a savoury sauce.

Noodles are widely eaten, usually with broth, often from little street stalls. Brown *soba* noodles are made from buckwheat and wheat flour. *Udon* are more like soft

A 'set' or fixed-price meal served in traditional lacquerware

spaghetti. *Ramen* are Chinese noodles served in a hot chicken or pork bone soup.

Restaurants (Ya)

Restaurants tend to specialise in one type of cuisine. *Kaiseki* is the most sophisticated and expensive style and is served in *ryotei*. In *okonomiyaki-ya* you will be served savoury pancakes and in *yakitori-ya*, skewers of chicken. *Teppanyaki* restaurants cook mainly steaks and *robatayaki-ya* specialise in rural 'home' cooking. Other restaurants specialise in eels, perhaps, or *fugu* (blowfish), which is very poisonous but tastes delicious. Menus are usually in Japanese, but many restaurants have plastic versions of their dishes in the window.

Drink

Green tea is widely drunk and is often served with meals. *Sake* (rice wine) is drunk warm with meals in the winter and with crushed ice in the summer. Japanese beer is very popular and good.

Eating noodles with relish is said to add to the flavour

Sake, invitingly sold in traditional bottles.

Horyuji Temple
Horyuji-mae
Daily 8–4:30
52, 60, 97, 98
Cheap

Kofukuji Temple
Nara-koen
Daily 9–4:30
1, 2
Moderate

Toshodaiji Temple
Yakushi-ji Higashiguchi
Daily 8:30–4:30
52, 97, 98
Cheap

NARA ✪✪✪

Nara is the oldest Japanese capital and the cradle of Japanese culture. Founded in 710 as Japan's first permanent capital, the old town is quite small, largely taken up by Nara Park, where many of the main attractions, and a lot of deer, reside. The town is compactly laid out, so nearly everything can be seen on foot.

One of the most famous sights is the Todaiji Temple with its Great Buddha (▶ 25). The **Horyuji Temple** complex houses what are probably the world's oldest surviving wooden buildings, whilst the vermilion Kasuga Taisha Shrine, rebuilt every 20 years in Heian style from the 8th until the 19th century, was designed to be the

Above: a dragon at one of the oldest intact temples in Japan – the Horyuji, Nara
Right: ferocious guardians at a temple entrance remind worshippers of their fragile mortality

guardian shrine of the capital. The temple area, filled with thousands of stone and bronze lanterns, is often the site of sacred dance performances. The **Kofukuji Temple** (Happiness-Producing Temple) was constructed as a school for the children of the Fujiwara family. It contains a 14th-century five-storey pagoda, the subject of a famous view from across the lake.

The Nara Museum houses a particularly fine collection of ancient Buddhist art. For many visitors the loveliest of Nara temples is the **Toshodaiji**, which dates back to 759 – its main hall and its religious lecture halls are considered national treasures.

Horyuji Temple, founded in AD 607, is the oldest intact temple complex in Japan

Did you know ?

There are three types of Japanese script. The basic script is called kanji *and was introduced from China. To allow for the differences between Chinese and Japanese grammar, a supplementary script called* hiragana *was devised. Finally* katakana *has been created for words with foreign origins..*

OKAYAMA ✪

A large city on the Inland Sea, Okayama is famous above all for **Korakuen Garden**, considered one of Japan's three famous gardens. Built between 1687 and 1700, the garden consists of 11ha of streams, bamboo groves, pine trees, cherry and plum – in short, a perfect miniaturised landscape. Okayama Castle (called Crow Castle because of its colour) houses an interesting display of armour.

✚ 64B2
✉ 170km west of Kyoto
🚉 Direct link to Osaka
✈ Regular flights to Tokyo
ℹ Okayama Station
   ☎ (086) 222 2912
❓ Saidiji Festival 3rd Sat in Feb

Korakuen Garden
✉ Shiroshita
🕐 Daily 7:30–6, Oct–Mar 8–5
🚋 Higashiyama tram to Shiroshita stop
♿ None
💴 Cheap

The serene beauty of Korakuen (the 'garden for taking pleasure later')

69

64C2
 30km south of Kyoto
Direct links to Kyoto, Tokyo and Beppu, Kobe, Kyushu, Shanghai
Osaka Itami (domestic) and Kansai (international)
Osaka Station ☎ (06) 6345 2189
Festivals: Otaue Shinji 14 Jun. Danjiri Matsuri 14–15 Sep

Osaka Castle
Otemon Gate, Osaka Castle Park
Daily 9–5:30, 15 Jul–31 Aug 9–8; Dec–Feb 9–4:30
Tanimachi-yonchome on Chuo or Tanimachi lines
Few   Moderate

Poster advertising a bunraku show

OSAKA   ★★

Japan's third largest city is utterly modern. It has little in the way of sights but is a fascinating place to wander about in, to discover the way of life of Osakan *shiminteki*, or 'people free of pretension', as locals like to call themselves. The city's best known landmark is the strategically sited **Osaka Castle**, which was built by Toyotomi Hideyoshi in 1583 and used as his headquarters. After his death, Tokugawan armies captured the castle, and it was further damaged in the fighting that led to the Meiji Restoration in 1868. The main gate and several towers have survived, however, and the main stronghold was rebuilt in 1931; further extensive renovation was carried out in 1997. Inside the castle is a museum; and there are fine views across the surrounding park to the city.

Osaka is something of a showplace for modern architecture, of which notable examples are the white towers of the Kirin Plaza on Ebisu Bridge, designed by Shin Takamatsu, and the Umeda Sky Building. Interesting to walk around at night is the Shinsaibashi/Dotombori area – you can admire its restaurants decorated with giant crustaceans and vegetables. Amerika-Mura is also worth a wander for its fashion shops, while the Museum of Oriental Ceramics in Kita-ku, which has more than a thousand exhibits, is considered to be one of the finest in the world.

Osaka is the centre for traditional *bunraku* (puppetry) theatre, which has been popular since the 17th century. Puppets, about two-thirds human size, perform a love story or historical tale, each puppet handled by three puppeteers. The chief puppeteer (and it takes about 30 years to become an expert) manipulates the puppet's head, eyes, mouth and right arm and hand. Catch a performance at the National Bunraku Theatre in Chuo-ku. Also well worth a visit is the impressive Osaka Aquarium (► 110) where you can see huge whale sharks.

Umeda, the hub of
Osaka's fashioned
department stores

A fish performs a
somersault on the eaves
of Osaka Castle

71

64B1

Train services between Kochi, Matsuyama, Takamatsu. Shinkansen from Yokohama, Tokyo

Regular flights from Takamatsu and Kochi to Fukuoka, Osaka and Tokyo

Regular ferries from Uno or Yokohama or from Tokyo or Osaka

Matsuyama Station
☎ (089) 931 3914

Kompira-san Shrine,
South of Kotohira
Daily 8–4
JR Dosan Line
Cheap

Below: *statue of Kobo Daishi at Takamatsu Temple*
Right: *imperial chrysanthemum emblem at Zentsuji Temple*

SHIKOKU ✪✪

The smallest of Japan's main islands lies off the San-yo coast of Honshu, and is linked to it by the Seto-Ohashi road and rail bridge, opened in 1988. A mountainous, wooded island, traditionally off the beaten track, there is nonetheless quite a lot to see here. The main town is Matsuyama, well known for its hot-spring public baths, Dogo Onsen. Matsuyama-jo, one of the best medieval castles in the country, stands on a hill in the middle of the town. Takamatsu, the main entry point to the island, is famous for the 17th-century Ritsurin Park, a charming maze of tea houses, ponds and islands; Zentsuji Temple, founded by Buddhist monk Kukai (Kobo Daishi) in AD 813 and the 75th station of the 88 Temple Circuit; and for Shikoku-mura village, an outdoor museum of old buildings.

One of the main attractions of Shikoku is the **Kompira-san Shrine**, revered across the country as the home of the protector of travellers and sailors; to reach it, pilgrims must brave a steep climb up 785 steps. Kochi is the home of one of Japan's few castles that have not been reconstructed (dating from 1603), and Uwajima also has an original castle.

A Cycle Ride in Shikoku

This is a pretty route which begins at the port of Imabari (served by regular ferries from Mihara on Honshu) and takes you to the spa town of Matsuyama.

From the port head in to the centre of Imabari.

This industrial town overlooks part of the Inland Sea noted for the whirlpools between its islets.

Turn left and head south on Route 317 and join the 196 to pass, after about 10km, through Toyo. A short distance after Toyo turn right on to Route 11. After about 4km, bear right on to the road for Tambara. About 7km later this road stops at a junction.

On your left, to the south, look out for Mount Ishizuchi, which, at 1,982m, is the highest point in western Honshu.

Distance
40km

Time
6hrs

Start point
Imabari
➕ 64B2

End point
Matsuyama
➕ 64B1

Lunch
Toyo

Turn left and continue to Sekiya. Turn right here and head up over a steep pass and descend to Shingenobu. Turn right on to Route 11. Bear right for some 3km and then right again onto a smaller road leading to Matsuyama.

You will pass a number of *onsen* before reaching Matsuyama, where the most famous of hot baths, the delightful Dogo Onsen, awaits.

Dogo Onsen hot baths, Matsuyama, where the emperor had a personal bath built

64B2

150km northwest of Kyoto

Direct links to Okayama and Tsuwano

Tottori Station ☎ (087) 223 318

64A2

350km west of Kyoto

Tsuwano Station on Yamaguchi JR line. Steam train from Agori ☎ (082) 264 5725 (book well in advance)

Tsuwano Station ☎ (0856) 72 1144

Sagi Mai Festival 20 and 27 July

Taikodani Inari Shrine

0.75km south of railway station

Daily

None

Cheap

Tsuwano's beautiful setting is best appreciated from the lofty heights of the castle

TOTTORI ✪

Located on the west coast, Tottori is of interest mainly for one thing – the expanse of sand dunes that were used as the film location for Teshigahara Hiroshi's classic 1964 film, *Woman in the Dunes*. The dunes lie, sometimes as much as a couple of kilometres wide, about 2km outside the city and stretch for 10km. There is a lookout and cable-car on the hillside behind.

TSUWANO ✪✪

A small mountain town of great charm, Tsuwano is famous above all as the home of the **Taikodani Inari Shrine**. The spectacular approach up steep steps passes beneath almost 2,000 red *torii* (gates). The ruins of the 14th-century Tsuwano Castle, high above the town, are reached by foot or chairlift. In the town itself water channels, filled with carp, line some of the streets of the old *samurai* quarter of Tonomachi. The former residences of the novelist Mori Ogai and the Meiji Restoration politician Nishi Amane are in the south of the town. Tsuwano can be reached via the picturesque steam train line from Ogori.

Did you know ?

The Japanese tend to avoid making direct statements, no matter how trivial they might seem to Westerners. Foreigners need to learn to look for indirect instructions – if, for example, it is time to leave, this might be expressed by a pointed reference to a waiting car.

Sunset over the rocky Kii Peninsula, Wakayama

WAKAYAMA

This remote prefecture on the Kii Peninsula is known for the Buddhist monasteries of Koya-san (▶ 65), the pilgrim trail known as the Kumanokodo, fine scenery and, in its southern part, hot springs. The best hot springs, some of which are open air, are located at Totsukawa, Yunomine (try Tsuboyu Onsen, where the water supposedly changes colour seven times a day), Kawayu (best in winter, when the entire river is turned into a huge hot bath), Watarase and Shirahama (with its superb white sand beach). As for scenery, the Dorokyo Gorge, which can be visited by boat, is considered the most impressive in Japan. The journey through the gorge in glass-roofed boats starts from Shiko and lasts about two hours, with regular daily departures between 9AM and 2PM. It is also worth a trip to admire the coastline around Cape Shiono-Misaki, once an island, but now linked to the Kii peninsula by a sandbar. This is now the foundation of the city of Kushimoto, but is most famous for a column of rocks likened to a procession of monks, called the Hashi-kuiiwa. The island of Kii Oshima, a short distance east of Kushimoto and linked to it by ferry, also has a beautiful coastline.

The Kumanokodo is an old pilgrimage road linking the three ancient holy shrines of Hongu, Nachi and Hayatama that today makes a pleasant hiking route.

YAMAGUCHI ✪

This pleasant town acted as capital during the tumultuous period between 1467 and 1573. There are a number of interesting sights, in particular the Xavier Memorial Chapel, which commemorates the visit of the Jesuit missionary in 1550 (recently rebuilt after a fire), and the Joeiji Temple with its beautiful Zen garden. In the Kozan-koen Park is a 15th- century pagoda, picturesquely situated beside a lake.

🚏 64C2
✉ 100km south of Kyoto
🚍 Direct link from Wakayama town to Osaka
ℹ️ International Exchange Section of Wakayama Prefectural Government
☎ (0734) 324 111

Graveyard at Koya-san, near Wakayama town

🚏 64A2
🚍 Direct link to Hagi
🚉 JR Yamaguchi line to Ogori
ℹ️ Yamaguchi Station
☎ (083) 933 0090

Kyushu & the Southern Islands

Kyushu, with its beautiful scenery and smoking volcanoes, may be considered the birthplace of Japanese history. According to legend, the wind god Ninigi began his rule of Japan here, which is perhaps a metaphorical reference to the earliest migrations from continental Asia. For many years Kyushu was the only link between Japan and the outside world, when the Dutch established a settlement at Nagasaki. There is a lot to enjoy here; above all, Nagasaki should not be missed, nor the dramatic countryside around Mount Aso.

The myriad islands to the south take you to another world entirely – clear tropical seas and fine beaches do not form part of the traditional picture of Japan. Perhaps the most famous island is Okinawa, with its splendid scenery, excellent nightlife and dramatic recent history.

> ' … yt being one of the fairest
> and lardgest harbours that eaver
> I saw, whereinto a man may
> enter in and goe out with
> shipping at all tymes '

RICHARD COCKS (on Nagasaki),
Letter to the East India Company
(1620)

———————●———————

Ferry ploughing towards Sakura-jima from Kagoshima

Nagasaki

Before the events of 9 August 1945 Nagasaki was best known as a picturesque port on Kyushu, which, for centuries before the Meiji Restoration, had acted as Japan's only link with the Western world.

On 9 August the second atomic bomb was dropped on the city, bringing World War II firmly to a close. The bomb missed its main target, the Mitsubishi shipyard, hitting instead a residential suburb, killing 75,000 people then, and the same number since as a result of wounds or the after-effects of radiation. Miraculously, some of the city survived and there remains quite a lot to see.

Nagasaki's links with the West began with the unplanned arrival of a Portuguese ship to Kyushu in 1542, to be followed by a visit by the missionary St Francis Xavier in 1549. These early contacts led to the establishment of Nagasaki port in 1571. The Portuguese began a profitable trade here, but soon Christianity began to be seen as a threat to the country's stability and was banned. The Portuguese were expelled to be replaced by the Dutch, who seemed to the Japanese to be traders rather than proselytisers. A small Dutch enclave survived the Edo period, and when this era came to an end Nagasaki soon consolidated its position as one of Japan's major ports.

The tram is the way to travel in Nagasaki

Spectacles Bridge is one of several to survive the atomic bomb

Decorated article of war in the Dejima Museum, Nagasaki

What to See in Nagasaki

DEJIMA

From the mid-17th century until 1855, Dejima was the site of the Dutch enclave, on a man-made island in Nagasaki harbour. Most traces of the settlement have gone, but the museum here tells its story, of how the Dutch traded Japanese goods for Western knowhow. There is also an outdoor model (one-fifth scale) of the old settlement.

82B4
Dejima
9–5. Closed Mon
Dejima tram
Few
Free

FUKUSAIJI ZEN TEMPLE/
NAGASAKI KANNON UNIVERSAL TEMPLE

Also known as the A-Bomb Martyrs Memorial, this faintly bizarre construction stands on the site of a temple originally built in 1628 but which was destroyed by the atomic bomb. Its replacement is in the form of a massive turtle carrying an image of the goddess Kannon. Inside is a huge Foucault pendulum (which demonstrates the angle of tilt of the earth's rotation). At 11:02 each day a bell rings out in remembrance of the bomb explosion.

82B4
300m east of Nagasaki Station
Daily
None
Cheap

GLOVER GARDENS

This open-air museum on a hillside overlooking the city features Western-style houses dating from the Meiji period. The museum takes its name from the oldest Western building in Japan, Glover Mansion, built by Scotsman Thomas Glover in 1863. The mansion is set in a pleasant park, and there are escalators to take you up to the top to enjoy the views.

82B4
Oura-Tenshudoshita
Daily, Mar–Nov 8–6; Dec–Feb 8:30–5
Tram 5, Oura-Tenshudoshita stop
None
Moderate

> ### *Did you know ?*
>
> *Although Japan is a highly advanced country technologically speaking, with over 95 per cent of Japanese companies having computers and fax machines, over a million people each year take the proficiency exams in the use of the soroban, or abacus.*

82B4
Daily 8–5
Tram 1, 4 to Kokaido-mae
None
Cheap

82B4
2km north of Nagasaki Station
Daily
Tram 1, 3 to Matsuyama-cho
None
Cheap

A-Bomb Museum
Daily 8:30–5
None
Cheap

KOFUKUJI AND SOFUKUJI TEMPLES   ✪✪

Both temples are located in the eastern part of central Nagasaki. Kofukuji is a revered Obaku-Zen temple built in Chinese Ming Dynasty style and is well known for its gardens, lawns and palms. Sofukuji is also Obaku-Zen and has a fine 17th-century gateway brought here from China in 1696. The route between the two is lined with a number of other smaller temples.

PEACE PARK   ✪✪

In remembrance of the atomic bomb dropped here in 1945, three times more powerful than the one dropped on Hiroshima, this park is located close to the site of the explosion and is dominated by the huge and rather ugly bronze Nagasaki Peace Statue; other statues have been donated by foreign nations. To the south of it is the **A-Bomb Museum**, which details the catastrophe and its appalling consequences.

Above: the Nagasaki Peace Statue

Right: a regal gateway to the Sofukuji Temple

Around Nagasaki

Start from the Hamano-machi Arcade, one of the city's main shopping areas, by the Daimaru department store.

Head east and at the end turn right to cross the tram line. At the junction of Kanko-dori with Shianbashi-dori, walk south (along Shianbashi-dori), through the heart of the Maruyuma entertainment area.

This was originally one of the few areas in the city where Dutch traders were allowed to have contact with the Japanese, although this contact was to be only in the form of trade and libidinous pleasures. The brothels have disappeared but it is still the centre for clubs and restaurants.

Continue to the first junction.

Opposite is the Fukusaya Castella Cake Shop, established in 1624, which sells cakes said to originate from recipes left behind by the Portuguese over 400 years ago. By turning left at the junction, a diversion will bring you to the historic Kagetsu Restaurant, a former pleasure house.

Return to the cake shop and bear left to continue to Chinatown.

During the Edo period the Chinese traders in Nagasaki settled here; only a very few buildings survive today, but the district still has an active Chinese community.

Northwest of Chinatown a tram can take you southwest to the escalators which lead up to Glover Gardens (▶ 79). Alternatively you can follow the tram route on foot (about 0.5 km).

The unmistakable gaudy glitter of a Chinese street

Distance
1.5km to Chinatown. 2km to Glover Garden

Time
1 hour

Start point
Daimaru Department Store

End point
Glover Gardens

Lunch
Various restaurants along Shianbashi-dori and in Chinatown

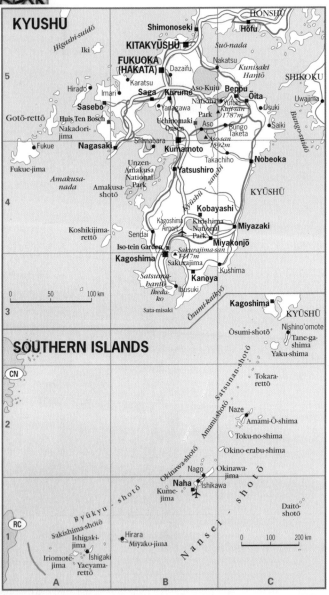

KYUSHU

Higashi-suidō
Iki
Hirado
Gotō-rettō
Sasebo
Huis Ten Bosch
Nakadori-jima
Fukue
Fukue-jima
Amakusa-nada
Amakusa-shotō
Koshikijima-rettō

Shimonoseki
KITAKYŪSHŪ
FUKUOKA (HAKATA)
Dazaifu
Karatsu
Imari
Saga
Kurume
Yanagawa
Uchinomaki Onsen
Shimabara
Nagasaki
Kumamoto
Unzen-Amakusa National Park
Yatsushiro
Kagoshima Airport
Sendai
Iso-tein Garden
Kagoshima
Sakurajima 1117m
Satsuma-hantō
Ikeda-ko
Ibusuki
Sata-misaki

HONSHŪ
Hōfu
Suō-nada
Nakatsu
Kunisaki Hantō
Aso-Kuju National Park
Beppu
Yufuin Ōita
Kuju-san 1787m
Usuki
Aso
Bungo Taketa
Aso-san 1592m
Takachiho
Kyūshū sanchi
Kobayashi
Kirishima National Park
Sakurajima-san
Sakurajima
Kushima
Kanoya
Ōsumi-kaikyō

SHIKOKU
Uwajima
Bungo-suidō
Saiki
Nobeoka
KYŪSHŪ
Miyazaki
Miyakonjō

0   50   100 km

Kagoshima
KYŪSHŪ
Nishino'omote
Tane-ga-shima
Yaku-shima

Ōsumi-shotō

SOUTHERN ISLANDS

CN

Satsunan-shotō
Tokara-rettō
Amami-shotō
Naze
Amami-Ō-shima
Toku-no-shima
Okino-erabu-shima
Okinawa-shotō
Nago
Okinawa-jima
Naha
Kume-jima
Ishikawa

Daitō-shotō

0   100   200 km

RC

Ryūkyū-shotō
Sakishima-shotō
Ishigaki-jima
Iriomote-jima
Ishigaki
Yaeyama-rettō
Hirara
Miyako-jima

Nansei-shotō

	A	B	C
5			
4			
3			
2			
1			

Kyushu Highlights

This drive takes you through the Kirishima-Yaku National Park, an area of ancient volcanoes and fine views.

Start from Kagoshima Airport and continue along the R504 for just over 5km. At Saikoji turn left onto the R223. Drive along here for about 7km to the Myoken hot springs, and then on to the hot-spring town of Makizono Maruo. From here turn left on to the Kirishima Skyline Road. After 10km you will reach Ebino-Kogen.

Ebino-Kogan is a pleasant stopping point for a walk or to admire the views. It is especially noted for wild flowers.

Distance
200km

Time
6 hours

Start/End point
Kagoshima Airport
✚ 82B3

Lunch
✉ Shishi-Jaya, Ikoma-Kogen. The speciality is game

Head for Kobayashi, reaching Ikoma Kogan after 15km. Continue, and at the Kobayashi interchange get on the Miyazaki motorway, leaving it again at the Takahara interchange. Take the R223 for 25km towards Kirishima.

The Kirishima-Jingu shrine is worth a visit. Originating from the 6th century but rebuilt in the 18th, it is in a great location, with views to Kobayashi and Mount Sakurajima.

Take the R223 to Maruo and return to Saikoji. Continue, and at the junction with the R10, turn right in the direction of Kagoshima. Follow the coast, with views of Mount Sakurajima to Iso-teien.

At Iso-teien there is a beautiful garden (➤ 85).

From Iso take the R10 towards central Kagoshima and then the R3 to the motorway at the Kagoshima-Kita interchange. From here it is just over 30km to Kagoshima Airport.

Angry-looking Mount Sakurajima is an active reminder that the Japanese islands lie on a geological fault line

What to See in Kyushu & the Southern Islands

BEPPU ✪✪

82C5

266 from Aso and Kumamoto

Beppu is on the JR Nippo and Hohi lines

Foreign Tourist Information Office, Furosen Bldg ☎ (0977) 231 119

Located on the northeast coast of Kyushu, Beppu is a rather kitsch resort famous for its hot springs, known as Jigoku ('hells'). There are a large number of them, including Chino-ike Jigoku, where the water is red, Umi Jigoku with a simmering expanse of azure sea water, and Hon Bozu Jigoku with its bubbling mud pools. Macaque monkeys descend from Mount Takosaki for regular feeds. Beppu also boasts the Hinokan Sex Museum that features exhibits ranging from erotic art to wooden phalluses.

DAZAIFU ✪

82B5

Nishitetsu-Dazaifu. Change at Futsukaichi

Nishitetsu-Dazaifu Station ☎ (092) 925 1880

An ancient capital of Kyushu close to Fukuoka, Dazaifu has an interesting shrine (Temman-gu), dedicated to the god of Scholarship, Tenjin, which is very popular with students taking exams. There are also a number of pleasant temples, including the Konmyozenji Temple, which has one of the most beautiful Zen gardens in Japan.

FUKUOKA (HAKATA) ✪

82B5

Direct links from JR Hakata Station to Osaka, Tokyo

Ferry services to Okinawa, Tokyo

Fukuoka Airport

JR Hakata Station ☎ (092) 431 3003; also Fukuoka International Association Rainbow Plaza, IMS Building, Tenjin ☎ (092) 431 3003

Originally two cities – the merchant's quarter of Hakata and the *samurai* quarter of Fukuoka – modern Fukuoka is the biggest city on Kyushu. The modern shopping centre is dominated by the golden IMS Building, and the Nakasu area is one of the best in Japan for expensive nightlife. Fukuoka is also the site of Japan's oldest Zen temple, the Shofukuji, northwest of the station and open daily. The new Asian Art Museum shows the best of Asian art.

The gently steaming waters of the Beppu 'hells' (right) are drunk by visitors for their health-giving properties (inset)

> ### *Did you know?*
>
> *Although tea is widely drunk in a perfunctory fashion, the traditional tea ceremony, which was originally a meditative aid for monks, is an elaborate – affair – utensils are polished, a special room is used, flowers are carefully arranged and the garden primped. The tea is important but is only part of a harmonious and contemplative experience.*

Below left: *relaxing in the Kagoshima heat*
Below:*Satsuma potter at work; the porcelain from this region is usually glazed cloudy white*

HUIS TEN BOSCH ⭕⭕

This recreation of a Dutch town has at least to be admired for its thoroughness. It is not a model town but the real thing complete with canals, windmills, reclaimed land, a replica of the Dutch Royal Family residence, a cheese market, shops and so on. A living town, the aim is for the population eventually to reach 10,000. The town was constructed (on reclaimed land) as an experiment in environmental harmony, and a computer continuously monitors the conservation and recycling systems.

➕ 82A5
✉ 1-1 Huis Ten Bosch, Machi, Sabeso City
🕐 Daily 9AM–8PM
🚌 Direct links to Fukuoka, Kumamoto, Nagasaki
🚆 Direct train to Fukuoka and Nagasaki

KAGOSHIMA ⭕⭕⭕

Located on the southern coast of Kyushu, Kagoshima was for generations ruled by a single clan, the Shimazu. The Shimazu bequeathed to the city its loveliest attraction, the 17th-century Iso-teien Garden, with the sea and Mount Sakurajima as a backdrop. In the garden is the Shimazu Villa, famous for its gold-leaf lined rooms and the stream where *sake* was floated downstream to participants at poem parties – the poem had to be completed before the *sake* arrived. A short ferry ride from Kagoshima is the smoking volcano of Sakurajima, which erupts almost daily. It cannot be climbed, but there are lookout points.

➕ 82B3
🚆 Kagoshima and Nishi-Kagoshima Stations
🚢 Ferry to Okinawa
✈ Kagoshima Airport
ℹ JR Nishi-Kagoshima Station ☎ (099) 253 2500

In the Know

If you only have a short time to visit Japan, or would like to get a real flavour of the country, here are some ideas:

10
Ways to Be a Local

Learn to enjoy karaoke. A willingness to stand up and make a fool of yourself for the benefit of others is considered entertainment.

Shop till you drop. Any major city in Japan is filled with shops, and people love, at the very least, to see what's on offer.

Peel your fruit. Japanese people always peel grapes and apples before eating them.

Don't blow your nose in public. An old chestnut and one which is becoming less relevant, but still worth bearing in mind .

Eat unusual vegetables. The Japanese eat all sorts of things that Westerners would never consider trying – ferns and water-lilies for example.

Wear a mask if you have a cold. Many Japanese wear a sort of surgical mask if they catch a cold in winter.

Buy a lunch box (bento). Office workers often buy a boxed set lunch from local take-aways.

Don't stick your chopsticks upright in your rice. That is how offerings are made to the dead.

Remember that the taxi door often opens automatically and that you will fall out if you are leaning on it.

Do remove your shoes when walking on tatami mats and other places like temples and changing rooms in stores.

10
Good Places to Have Lunch

Cook's (££)
 Kenkyusha Eigo Centre Building, 1-2 Kagurazaka, Shinjuku-ku, Tokyo ☎ (03) 3235 9535. Restaurant serving British-style lunch with English beer.

Shin-Hokkaien (££)
 2F, 3-16-15 Roppongi, Minato-ku, Tokyo ☎ (03) 3505 881. Authentic Beijing restaurant with excellent dim sum.

Washtub boat driver, Sado-shima

Fisherman's Grill (££)
 Sunset Beach Restaurant Row, 1-3-5 Daiba, Minato-ku, Tokyo ☎ (03) 5531 5007 (O-daiba Kaihin Koen sta). Western seafood restaurant with great view of the beach and Rainbow Bridge.

Hinazushi Sushi Bar
 1-3-5 Daiba, Minato-ku, Tokyo ☎ (03) 5531 0017. One of a chain of sushi bars with excellent-priced menu offering 'all you can eat'.

Kikunoi (£££) 459 Shimo Kawaramachi, Yasaka Torii Mae, Shimo Kawaramachi-dori, Higashiyama-ku, Kyoto 605 ☎ (075) 561 0015. Japanese haute cuisine in traditional restaurant in the heart of one of Kyoto's most famous areas.

Sasaki (£) 139 Kurumajicho, Kamitkano, Sakyo-ku, Kyoto-shi, Kyoto ☎ (075) 712 7879. Inexpensive Japanese noodle restaurant. Closed Wed. English spoken.

Kawafune (££)
 Nagaragawa Hotel, 51-1 Nagara Ukaiya, Gifu-shi, Gifu-ken ☎ (058)232 4111. Japanese restaurant serving excellent set lunch. Some English spoken.

New Takeya Saloon (£)
 2-6-44 Nakadori, Akita-shi, Akita-ken ☎ (0188) 34 5521. Restaurant serving Japanese, Chinese and Western food with varied lunch specials. Closed first Mon of each month. English spoken.

Bistro D'Azur (££)
✉ 2-3-21 Shinsaibashi-suji, Chuo-ku, Osaka-shi, Osaka-fu ☎ (06) 211 4752. Mediterranean restaurant just 7min walk from Subway/Kintetsu Namba station, offering a special lunch menu at excellent prices. English spoken.

Okaru (£) ✉ 13 Higashimuki Nakamachi, Nara-shi, Nara-ken ☎ (0742) 24 3686. Restaurant specialising in *okonomiyaki*, a type of pancake whose name literally means 'cook to one's taste'. Customers select the ingredients from the menu and cook the pancakes themselves on a hotplate in the centre of the table. English spoken.

5
Top Activities

Going on a pilgrimage: most people in Japan lead at least a nominal religious life and visits to temples appropriate to a wish or a need continue to play an important role. More than that, for the serious follower of Buddhism, there are circuits to follow that will involve a round of visits to famous temples or long hikes up holy mountains.

Having communal baths: bathing is an important pastime in Japan among people of all ages. There are some 2,000 communal

Pilgrims' slippers for sale in Matsuyama

public baths (known as *sento*) in Tokyo alone. The system involves sitting on a small stool, soaping the body with a cloth and rinsing thoroughly so you are clean before immersing oneself in the communal hot bath.

Hiking: nearly all the national parks in Japan have hiking routes. Maps are readily available in hiking areas but are rarely in foreign languages. The most beautiful places for hiking are in the Japan Alps and in Hokkaido.

Martial arts: practised worldwide as forms of self-defence, Japanese martial arts come in many forms. Karate and judo are the most famous but there are many others, including *aikido* ('The Way of Harmony'), *kendo* ('The Way of the Sword') and *kyudu*, which is Japanese archery.

Watching a *sumo* match: the one sport that is associated with Japan and nowhere else is the esoteric form of wrestling called *sumo*. It is performed on a hard-packed clay circle, 4.5m in diameter, by huge, top-knotted specimens of Japanese manhood wearing nothing more than a sort of rigid loincloth with a fringe. Salt is thrown to purify the arena. The combatants square up to each other. One launches himself at the other. In the ensuing struggle the winner is he who shoves the other out of the ring. There are six annual tournaments in Osaka, Nagoya, Fukuoka

Noboribetsu Onsen, in Shikotsu-Toya National Park, Hokkaido

and Tokyo. *Sumo* is very popular, and the top wrestlers enjoy celebrity status.

10
Famous Hot Springs (*Onsen*)

- **Arima:** 1,300-year-old hot spring behind Mount Rokko, close to Osaka.
- **Arita Kanko Hotel:** hotel offering hot baths in a cable-car over dramatic coastal scenery.
- **Asakusa Kannon Onsen, Tokyo:** public bath with hot spring water.
- **Atami:** close to Tokyo and popular with tourists.
- **Beppu:** one of the most famous resorts in Japan – tacky but entertaining.
- **Dogo Onsen:** famous spa close to Matsuyama.
- **Hakone Onsen:** 14 hot springs with views of Mount Fuji.
- **Ibusuki Onsen, Kyushu:** bury yourself in hot sand and enjoy the steam from underground natural springs.
- **Noboribetsu Onsen, Hokkaido:** there are 11 types of spring water at this hot spring.
- **Sakino-yu Onsen, Shirahama** is built into rocks by the sea.

82B4

JR Kumamoto Station with links to Fukuoka, Miyazaki

Kumamoto Airport serves Okinawa, Osaka, Tokyo. 60min from town

JR Kumamoto Station
☎ (096) 352 3743

KUMAMOTO ★★

A large, modern city in the western heart of the island, Kumamoto has two principal attractions – its castle and a fine garden. The castle was once a splendid affair, with 49 turrets and 5km of outer walls. It was considered impregnable, but rebel *samurai* beseiged it for 55 days in 1877, finally succeeding in burning it to the ground. It was rebuilt to house the impressive treasury of the ruling Hosokawa clan. The 17th-century garden, Suizenji-koen Park, is a small-scale reconstruction of the old Tokaido road between Kyoto and Tokyo and features a miniature Mount Fuji.

82B1

Ferries from Miyako-jima to Ishigaki-jima and Okinawa

Regular flights from Miyako-jima to Okinawa, Naha, Tokyo, Osaka

MIYAKO ISLANDS ★★

This group of islands 300km southwest of Okinawa comprises Miyako-jima, Irabu-jima, Shimo-jima and a handful of smaller islands. Hirara is the capital of Miyako-jima but there is not very much to see here: the main attractions are the island's beaches, especially the Yonaha Mae-hama beach on the southwest coast.

MIYAZAKI ✪✪

A town with a year round sub-tropical climate and which was a traditional destination for honeymooners, Miyazaki is a pleasant place of palm-fringed avenues and a beautiful coastline that stretches to the south. It has an important shrine, the Miyazaki-jingu Shrine and Museum, dedicated to the mythical first emperor of Japan, Emperor Jimmu. The museum is devoted to local history and archaeology. The Heiwadai-koen Park, embellished with reproductions of clay figures from regional burial mounds, is worth a diversion.

➕ 82C4
✉ Southeast coast of Kyushu
🚆 Direct links by JR to Fukuoka, Kagoshima, Kumamoto
🚢 Ferry link to Osaka
ℹ JR Miyazaki Station
☎ (0985) 226 469
❓ Mid-Apr Furusato Festival

MOUNT ASO ✪✪✪

The Aso-Kuju National Park is in the middle of Kyushu between Beppu and Kumamoto and is not to be missed. Mount Aso is actually five volcanoes, of which the highest is Mount Takadake (1,592m), in the world's largest caldera (128km in circumference). Although one of the peaks, Mount Nakadake, is highly active, there is a cable-car to its summit. The peaks rise out of a landscape of green meadows that cover the floor of the caldera, creating an atmosphere that is at once bucolic and primeval. The cable-car runs from the Aso-zan Nishi ropeway station, which is 40 minutes from Aso town.

➕ 82B5
✉ 50km northeast of Kumamoto
🚆 From Aso JR Station to Aso-San Nishi ropeway, or direct from Kumamoto to Aso-nishi
🚆 Direct links to Beppu, Kumamoto
ℹ JR Aso Station
☎ (09676) 34 0751

Opposite top: *a landscape in miniature at Suizenji-koen Park, Kumamoto*
Opposite bottom: *tropical beaches line the Miyako Islands*
Left: *enjoy a lazy ride amid the wonderful scenery of the world's largest caldera on Mount Aso*

82B1

Services from Naha to Kagoshima, Nagoya, Osaka, Tokyo

Naha International

Palette Kumoji Bldg, Kokusai-dori, Naha

(098) 866 7515

Jiriuma festival, Naha, Mar. Hari boat races, May. Tsunahiki festival, Aug

Shuri-koen Park

3.5km east of Naha town centre

Daily 9–5

12, 13, 14, 17

Park: free. Castle, temples: moderate

82C3

Ferries from Tane-ga-shima and Yaku-shima to Kagoshima

From Tane-ga-shima and to Kagoshima

82A1

Ishigaki-jima

Regular flights from Ishigaki-jima to Okinawa

The ancient Ryukyu capital of Shuri, Okinawa

OKINAWA

The capital of this, the largest and most important island in the Nansei-shoto chain, is the colourful, relaxed city of Naha. The heart of Naha is Kokusai-dori, lined with shops and bars, to the south of which is the Tsuboya area of traditional pottery shops. About 3km east is Shuri, the ancient Ryukyu capital. Much of this was destroyed in World War II, but what remains is to be found in **Shuri-koen Park**, the highlights of which include Shuri Castle and the Shureimon Gate, and the 16th-century Kankaimon Gate. North of Naha are the atmospheric hilltop ruins of Nakagusuku Castle and Nakamuru House, a traditional Okinawan residence. The northern part of the island is the least spoilt – Oku is an interesting village of traditional Okinawan houses, and nearby Cape Hedo-misaki, the northernmost point, has spectacular views. Okinawa was the scene of terrible battles towards the end of World War II and there are several commemorative sites, notably at Himeyuri-To and Mabuni-no-Oka.

OSUMI-SHOTO ISLANDS

This group of islands in the Nansei-shoto chain is closest to Kyushu. There are two main islands, flat and agricultural Tane-ga-shima, the site of the first Portuguese landing in 1543, and volcanic Yaku-shima, whose 1,935m peak, Mount Miyanoura-dake, is the highest in southern Japan. There is good walking here among waterfalls and forests.

YAEYAMA ISLANDS

At the very southwestern tip of the Nansei-shoto archi-pelago, the Yaeyama islands consist of the main islands of Ishigaki-jima and Iriomote-jima (► 19) and a few smaller islands. On Ishigaki-jima the Yaeyama Minzoku-en Village specialises in pottery and weaving, and there are excellent beaches and diving sites.

Where To...

Above: *shopping is a national pastime*
Right: *Japanese children are always impeccably behaved*

Hokkaido &
Northern Honshu

Prices are approximate and are exclusive of drinks but inclusive of service:

£   = up to ¥2,500
££   = up to ¥9,000
£££ = over ¥9,000

You may occasionally find that you will be refused entry to certain restaurants. Such cases are rarely examples of discrimination, more a fear of not being able to cope with foreigners' demands.

Akita
Kamada Kaikan (£–££)
This restaurant serves both western and Japanese food in pleasant surroundings. The Japanese specialities are *kiritampo* (rice and chicken hotpot), *shottsuro* (hotpot with pickles) and a 'local speciality combo'. Some English spoken.
⊠ 4-16-4 Nakadori, Akita-shi ☎ (018) 832 2155 🕓 Lunch, dinner 🚉 JR Akita Station

Hakodate
Bay Restaurant (££)
Interesting seafood dishes, such as tuna fish in coconut milk, are served here in a waterfront warehouse.
⊠ 11-5 Toyokawa-cho ☎ (0138) 221 300 🕓 Lunch, dinner

Chat Noir (£)
A restaurant serving good, inexpensive Japanese food in modern, relaxing surroundings.
⊠ Union Square, Meijikan ☎ (0138) 271 200 🕓 Lunch, dinner

Raj Morita (£)
If you want a change from Japanese food, this is a good place for reasonably priced Indian cooking.
⊠ 32-29 Honcho, Hakodate-shi ☎ (0138) 561 991 🕓 Lunch, dinner. Closed Wed 🚋 Honcho streetcar

Hirosaki
Kagi-nohana (£)
Although it is not in a particularly attractive location, this restaurant is well worth visting for its delicious local specialities, including river fish.
⊠ East Building 2, Kagimachi 🕓 Dinner

Kanazawa
Kaga Tobi (£)
Located in a quiet, central street just to the north of the river, the Kaga Tobi serves a good mixture of Japanese cooking styles.
⊠ Kohrinbo 109, 2-1 Kohrinbo ☎ (076) 262 0535 🕓 Dinner

Kanko Bussankan (£)
Close to the main gate of the Kenrokuen Garden, this restaurant serves *ramen* (Chinese noodles) and *sashimi* (raw fish) as well as the local specialities of river fish, shrimps and mountain vegetables.
⊠ 2-20 Kenrokumachi ☎ (076) 222 7788 🕓 10–6 🚌 10, 11

Miyoshian (££)
This long-established restaurant located in the Kenrokuen Garden is in traditional surroundings and offers lovely views over the pond.
⊠ 1-11 Kenrokumachi ☎ (076) 221 0127 🕓 Lunch, dinner 🚌 10, 11

Tamazushi (£)
One of the best *sushi* restaurants in the locality and although there is no English menu you will have no problem in finding out what is on offer.
⊠ Katamachi 🕓 Dinner, closes at 8PM

Otaru
Takinami (£)
Close to the canal and with a relaxing atmosphere, Takinami specialices in reasonably priced fish sets, especially for lunch.
⊠ Otaru Canal area, close to Otaru Museum 🕓 Lunch, dinner

Sapporo

Hyosetsu-no-Mon (££)

Located in Susukino district, this restaurant is well-known for its crab dishes – in fact, every dish involves crab. Lively establishment with menu in English.

✉ S5W2 Sapporo
☎ (011) 521 3046 ⏱ Dinner
🚇 Susukino

Ramen Yokocho (£)

This is not a single restaurant but a whole small street of them, all specialising in the local favourite dish, *ramen*, Chinese noodles.

✉ Susukino ⏱ Lunch, dinner

Round Midnight (££)

Popular hotel restaurant which serves a mixture of Japanese, Chinese and Western dishes. Good value set meals or 'all-you-can-eat' choice.

✉ Hotel Arthur, S10W6, Sapporo ☎ (011) 561 1000
⏱ Lunch, dinner
🚇 Nakajima-koen

Sapporo Biru-en (££–£££)

This is the original brewery of the Sapporo Beer Company, which has been converted into a brasserie or *bier keller*. The main thing to eat with the beer is a Mongolian barbecue, known in this restaurant as 'Genghis Khan'.

✉ N6 E9, Higashi 9-chome, Higashi-ku ☎ (011) 742 1531
⏱ Lunch, dinner

Silo (££)

This restaurant, in an old barn-like building, serves local specialities such as sliced frozen salmon, bear meat and smoked deer.

✉ 5 Minamo, 3 Nishi Chou-ku,
Susukino ☎ (011) 531 5837
⏱ Lunch, dinner

Yamasa Kaikan (££)

Excellent Japanese food in several styles including *oden* (ingredients, especially tofu and yam, simmered in soy and kelp stock), *sushi* (rice and savoury pieces) and *yakitori* (grilled chicken). Prices are moderate and some English is spoken.

✉ 7-2-11 2-jo, Kotoni, Nishiku
☎ (011) 621 2706 ⏱ Dinner.
Closed Sun and holidays
🚇 Kotoni

Sendai

Aobajo-Honmarukaikan (£)

Fairly central, the eatery specialises in *teishoku*, which is a set meal consisting of a main dish, a soup, Japanese pickles and rice or bread.

✉ Aobajoushi, Tenshudai, Aoba-ku ☎ (022) 222 0218
⏱ Daily 9–5
🚇 Aobajoushiato Sendai bus stop

Iwashiya (££)

A traditional establishment with *tatami* seating, this is thought to be the best seafood restaurant in the city.

✉ 4-5-42 Ichiban-cho
☎ (022) 222 6645 ⏱ Dinner

Sendai Kakitoku (£)

Specialises in seafood especially *kaki don* (oysters with *miso* soup and pickled vegetables) and *kakitoku teishoku* (a 'set' that includes fried oysters with rice and three other dishes).

✉ 4-9-1 Ichiban-cho, Aoba-ku
☎ (022) 222 0785 ⏱ Lunch, dinner. Closed Mon
🚇 Koutoudaikouen

Best Guest

If invited to a meal in Japan, it is the host's job to order on your behalf, and in a restaurant it's easier and more respectful to allow the host to choose what you will eat. When the meal arrives, diners usually murmur the Japanese equivalent of *bon appetit,* which is *itadakimasu.* It means 'I will receive'.

Central Honshu

Follow the Sign

Types of restaurant can be distinguished by various signs. A *shabu-shabu* or *sukiyaki* (➤ 66) restaurant will display a drawing of a cow, a *fugu* restaurant a dangling blowfish, and a *yakitori* (➤ 67), *oden* (a dish of tofu, seaweed, fish cakes and similar ingredients boiled in fish stock) or *izakaya* (similar to a Western pub) establishments a red lantern. Others will have curtains with the type of restaurant indicated in Japanese.

Matsumoto

Hanakurabe (£)

Some English is spoken in this restaurant, which specialises in *tempura*-style prawns with vegetables on a bowl of rice, and *Hanakurabe gozen*, the speciality of the house.

✉ 1F Hotel Buena Vista, 1-2-1 Honjo ☎ (0263) 370 511 🕐 Lunch, dinner 🚉 JR Matsumoto

Shizuka (£)

A restaurant that serves very reasonably priced 'sets' (*teishoku*) including *oden teishoku* (soup made of seaweed broth with bits of steamed fish paste).

✉ 4-10-8 Ote ☎ (0263) 320 547 🕐 Lunch, dinner (dinner only Mon). Closed Sun

Nagano

Otaya (£)

A restaurant specialising in home-made *soba* – thin buckwheat noodles sometimes flavoured with green tea, which are often served in soy-based broth.

✉ Chuo-dori 🕐 Lunch

Nagoya

Kishimen-tei (£)

One of the specialities of the region is *kishimen* noodles and this restaurant is renowned for serving them at tolerable prices.

✉ 3-20-4 Nishiki, Naka-ku ☎ (052) 951 3481 🕐 Lunch, dinner

Unazen (£ ££)

This restaurant specialises in eel dishes – *unadon* is eel served on rice, whilst *unajuu* is grilled eel with a sweet soy sauce.

✉ 1-17-26 Meieki Minami, Nakamura-ku ☎ (052) 551 5253

🕐 Lunch, dinner. Closed Sun 🚉 JR Nagoya Station

Yaegaki Tempura (££)

A restaurant that has been around for a long time and is located in an old wooden building. It specialises in fish and vegetable *tempura*. English spoken.

✉ 3-17-28 Nishiki, Naka-ku ☎ (52) 951 3250 🕐 Lunch, dinner

Takayama

Kakusho (££–£££)

A famous restaurant in an old house near the Tenshoji Temple well-known for *shojin-ryori*, which is Buddhist vegetarian food.

✉ 2-98 Babacho ☎ (0577) 320 174 🕐 Lunch, dinner

Kofune (£)

A small and convenient restaurant near the station that serves various noodle dishes. There is an English menu.

✉ Hanasato-cho 6-6 ☎ (0577) 322 106 🕐 Lunch

Suzuya (£–££)

Located in the centre of the town, Suzuya is a small country-style restaurant serving local specialities such as *ayu* (river fish), *hida-soba* (noodles) and *sansai-ryori* (mountain vegetables). English-language menu available.

✉ 24 Hanakawacho ☎ (0577) 322 484 🕐 Lunch, dinner

Tokyo

Daikokuya (£)

Only three meat dishes are served – *shabu-shabu* (beef and vegetable hotpot), *sukiyaki* (stir-fried beef, bean curd and vegetables) and *yakiniku* (grilled meats) – and you can eat as much as you like for a set price within a given time limit.

✉ **Naka-dai Bldg, 4th Fl, 1-27-5 Kabuki-cho** ☎ **(03) 3202 7272** 🕐 **Dinner** 🚇 **Shinjuku, east exit**

Ginza Benkay (££–£££)

This restaurant serves a variety of Japanese styles of cooking – *sushi, shabu-shabu* and *teppanyaki* (where ingredients are fried on a hot plate at the table) – each in its own area furnished with wood, bamboo and screens.

✉ **7-2-17 Ginza** ☎ **(03) 3573 7335** 🕐 **Lunch, dinner** 🚇 **Hibiya or Yurakucho**

Hayashi (££–£££)

A small restaurant with relaxing, rustic decoration, specialising in grilled Japanese food, which is prepared by the customer at his own *hibachi*. The lunch menu is *oyakodomburi* (rice, egg and chicken).

✉ **Sanno Kaikan Bldg, 4thFl, 2-14-1 Akasaka** ☎ **(03) 3582 4078** 🕐 **Lunch, dinner (dinner only Sat). Closed Sun** 🚇 **Akasaka**

Irohanihoheto (£)

This is a *yakitori* restaurant and also a tavern that serves Western dishes. It tends to attract young people, probably because the food is good and very reasonably priced.

✉ **1-19-3 Jinnan, Shibuya-ku** ☎ **(03) 3476 1682** 🕐 **Dinner** 🚇 **Shibuya**

Kana-Uni (£–££)

Established over thirty years ago, this restaurant serves Franco-Japanese food with dishes such as grilled fish and poached fillet of sole with sea-urchin sauce. There is live jazz in the evenings.

✉ **1-1-16 Moto-Akasaka** ☎ **(03) 3404 4776** 🕐 **Dinner** 🚇 **Akasaka-mitsuke**

Kisso (££–£££)

The restaurant, with modern but comfortable decoration, is in a building with shops selling gourmet cooking utensils. *Kaiseki*-style (*haute cuisine*) Japanese food is served.

✉ **Axis Bldg, 5-17-1 Roppongi** ☎ **(03) 3582 4191** 🕐 **Lunch, dinner. Closed Sun** 🚇 **Roppongi**

Komagata Dojo (££)

An old-fashioned restaurant established for over 180 years. It sells set meals (*teishoku*) but specialises in *dojo*, which is a small river fish. Customers all sit on *tatami* mats.

✉ **1-7-12 Komagata, Taito-ku** ☎ **(03) 3842 4001** 🕐 **Lunch, dinner** 🚇 **Asakusa**

Selan (££)

Here, in what bears a passing resemblance to a French bistro, the food is so-called *nouvelle Japonaise*, which is essentially Western-style cooking using traditional Japanese ingredients.

✉ **2-1-19 Kita-Aoyama** ☎ **(03) 3478 2200** 🕐 **Lunch, dinner** 🚇 **Aoyama-Itchome or Gaienmae**

Yabu Soba (£)

In business for over a century, and situated in a small bamboo garden, this is one of Tokyo's most famous *soba* noodle shops. There is a menu in English.

✉ **2-10 Awajicho, Kanda** ☎ **(03) 3831 4728** 🕐 **Lunch, dinner** 🚇 **Awajicho**

Yokohama

Su-u-ro Saikan

Many of the best Chinese restaurants are to be found along Yamashitacho, this one among them. English is spoken.

✉ **190 Yamashitacho, Naka-ku** ☎ **(045) 681 3456** 🕐 **Lunch, dinner** 🚇 **JR Ishikawacho**

Tofu

Tofu (soya bean curd) is not only nutritious but infinitely versatile – it can be boiled, fried, baked or eaten fresh. Tofu is made by soaking soya beans, extracting the 'milk' and then curdling it; it is sold on the day of production. The best tofu is said to come from Kyoto.

Western Honshu & Shikoku

Cheers!

The Japanese word for drinking each other's health is *kanpai*, the literal meaning of which is 'to an empty cup' or 'bottoms up'. An empty cup or glass signals to the host that you want more to drink. If you have had a surfeit, leave your glass full.

Hagi
Fujita Soba-ten (£)

A welcoming restaurant that specialises in home-made *soba* and also in *tempura*.

✉ Kumagai-cho ☎ (0838) 221 086 🕐 Lunch, early dinner. Closed 2nd and 4th Wed of each month

Hiroshima
Suishin (£–££)

This restaurant on five floors specialises in *kamameshi*, which is a savoury rice pudding cooked with a number of ingredients, including fresh fish.

✉ 6-7 Tatemachi, Naka-ku ☎ (082) 247 4411 🕐 Lunch, dinner

Kobe
Misono (££–£££)

An old restaurant that is very well known for the quality of its steaks, which come from locally bred cattle. The steaks are cooked at your table.

✉ 1-7-6 Kitanagasa-dori ☎ (078) 331 2890 🕐 Dinner

Kyoto
Daiichi (£££)

Famous for its turtle dishes, which have been cooked here for 12 generations and which are considered warming in the winter.

✉ 6-371, Shimochojamachi, Senbon Nishiiru, Kamigyo-ku ☎ (075) 461 1775 🕐 Lunch, dinner

Doi (££–£££)

Situated at the foot of the Higashiyama hills and offering good views of the city, this restaurant has served *kaiseki* cooking since 1938.

✉ 353 Kodaiji, Masuyacho, Higashiyamaku ☎ (075) 561 0309 🕐 Lunch, dinner. Reservations required

Fujiya (££–£££)

This famous restaurant located close to the Kibune Shrine specialises in fish in the summer (with dining platforms by the river) and *botan nabe* (wild boar) in the winter.

✉ 40 Kibunecho, Kurama, Sakyo-ku ☎ (075) 741 2501 🕐 Lunch, dinner

Gombei (£–££)

Close to the Gion Corner Theatre, this good-value restaurant specialises in noodle and rice dishes. A particular favourite is roasted *anago* (sea eel).

✉ 254 Gion-machi, Kitagawa, Higashiyama-ku ☎ (075) 561 3350 🕐 Lunch, dinner. Closed Thu

Hanbe Fu (£–££)

This restaurant near the Gojo Bridge specialises in *fu* (wheat gluten) cooking – a branch of vegetarian cooking unique to Kyoto – and has done so for over 300 years.

✉ Minimazume, Gojo Ohashi Higashi, Higashiyama-ku ☎ (075) 525 0008 🕐 Lunch. Closed Sun. Reservations required

Hyotei (££–£££)

Formerly a tea shop, this restaurant has a 300-year-old entranceway and attractive thatched building overlooking a garden and pond. Fairly expensive *kaiseki* and traditional Kyoto cooking.

✉ 35 Kusakawa-cho, Nanzenji Sakyo-ku ☎ (075) 771 4116 🕐 Lunch, dinner. Closed 2nd and 4th Tue each month

Isecho (£££)

Established since 1715, the interior is in the *sukiya* architectural style. The

cooking is *kaiseki*, using seasonal ingredients and served on fine ceramic ware.
✉ **387 Mukadeyacho, Shinmachi, Nishikikoji-agaru** ☎ **(075) 221 0300** 🕐 **Lunch, dinner**

Misoka-ankawamichiya (£)
Probably the most famous *soba* noodle shop in the city, with small rooms around a central courtyard. It's been here for 300 years.
✉ **Fuyacho-dori, Sanjo-agaru** ☎ **(075) 221 2525** 🕐 **Lunch, early dinner**

Tenki (££–£££)
In a beautiful garden, convenient for the Nijo Castle, this restaurant serves food in both traditional and modern dining styles. Specialities include *tempura* and delicate Japanese *kaiseki*. Some English spoken.
✉ **89 Jozenjicho, Senbon Imadegawaagaru, Kamigyoku** ☎ **(075) 461 4146** 🕐 **Lunch, dinner. Closed 2nd and 4th Mon of each month**

Umenoi (££)
Established in Gion for over 80 years, this restaurant has a comfortable atmosphere and specialises in eel dishes and traditional local dishes. English menu available.
✉ **160 Shijoagaru Joubanmachi, Yamatoji-dori, Higashiyama-ku** ☎ **(075) 561 1004** 🕐 **Lunch, dinner. Closed Wed**

Matsue
Minami-kan (££)
A modern restaurant serving high-quality *kaiseki* cooking, as well as local specialities from a seasonal menu.
✉ **14 Suetsugu Honmachi** ☎ **(0852) 215131** 🕐 **Lunch, dinner**

Matsuyama
Shin-Hamasku (££)
Located in the centre of the city, the Shin-Hamasku specialises in local dishes and fresh seafood.
✉ **Sanbancho-4-chome** ☎ **(089) 933 3030** 🕐 **Lunch, dinner**

Nara
Furusato (£–££)
A restaurant specialising in *udon* and *tempura* at very reasonable prices. English menu available.
✉ **10 Higashimuki Nakamachi** ☎ **(0742) 222 828** 🕐 **Lunch, dinner. Closed Tue** 🚉 **Kintetsu Nara**

Osaka
Agura (££)
A restaurant that serves high-quality charcoal-grilled cooking and specialises in horse-meat.
✉ **Namba** ☎ **(06) 212 1460** 🕐 **Dinner**

Fuguhisa (££)
As the name suggests, this restaurant specialises in the famous blow- or puffer fish (*fugu*). Prices are very good and the simply served food is excellent.
✉ **3-14-24 Higashi-ohashi, Higashinari-ku** ☎ **(06) 972 5029** 🕐 **Dinner**

Imai (£)
A very good-value restaurant specialising in *soba* and *udon* noodles at exceptional prices. English menu available.
✉ **1-7-22 Dotonbori, Chuo-ku** ☎ **(06) 211 0319** 🕐 **Lunch, dinner** 🚉 **Kintetsu Namba**

Kuidaore (£–££)
Like many restaurants in competitive Osaka, the Kuidaore tries to stand out from the crowd; in this case the attraction is a huge mechanical clown at the entrance. There are different types of Japanese food on four floors – the higher the floor the higher the price.
✉ **1-8-25 Dotonbori** ☎ **(06) 211 5300** 🕐 **Lunch, dinner**

Foreign Options
Korean (*yakinuku-ya*) restaurants are also popular throughout Japan. They feature marinated meat and vegetables which are grilled at the table and dipped into a spicy sauce. The meat served is usually beef, which is either *rousu* (lean cut) or *karubi* (ribs).

Kyushu & the Southern Islands

Chopsticks
Chopsticks are easier to manipulate than you might think. Hold the thick end of the sticks like a pen, with the lower stick resting in the cleft between thumb and finger and against the fourth finger. Hold the upper stick with the thumb and first two fingers. When picking up food, keep the lower stick still and manipulate the upper one.

Beppu

Amamijaya (£)
This restaurant is well known for its home-made noodles at good prices. It also serves *fugu*, the famous lethal puffer fish, whose poison is expertly removed by specially trained chefs.
✉ 1-4 Jissoji ☎ (0977) 676 024 🕐 Lunch, dinner

Fugumatsu (££)
As the name suggests, this restaurant specialises in *fugu*, or puffer fish. Also serves other good fish dishes.
✉ 3-6-14 Kitahama ☎ 0977 211 717 🕐 Dinner

Fukuoka

Gourmet City (£–£££)
A collection of restaurants offering something for all tastes and pockets, located in the basement of the Centraza Hotel.
✉ Centraza Hotel, 4-23 Hakataeki-Chuogai ☎ (092) 461 0111 🕐 Lunch, dinner 🚆 Hakata

Hemmingway's (£)
Late bar/pizza house with a friendly, relaxed atmosphere, offering excellent value.
✉ 2718 Maizuru, Tenjin ☎ (092) 751 5591 🕐 Lunch, dinner

Ichiki (£)
Relaxed and informal snack restaurant serving simple meat dishes and skewered fish.
✉ 1-2-10 Maizara, Chuo-Ku ☎ (092) 751 5591 🕐 Lunch, dinner

Tsukushino (£££)
Located high up in an hotel with tremendous views across the city, this restaurant serves high-quality Japanese food with prices to match.
✉ ANA Hotel, 3-3-3 Hakata-Ekimae ☎ (092) 471 7111 🕐 Lunch, dinner

Kagoshima

Satsuma (£)
A reasonably priced restaurant specialising in local 'satsuma'-style cooking, including *kibinago* (a sort of *sashimi*, ➤ 66) and *torisashi* (raw chicken with soy sauce).
✉ 27-30 Chuochu ☎ (099) 2522 661 🕐 Lunch, dinner

Kumamoto

Itchko (££)
Offering a considerable range of local specialities, the Itchko is a good, reliable restaurant located in a hotel only a short distance east of Kumamoto Castle.
✉ Kumamoto Castle Hotel ☎ (096) 326 3311 🕐 Lunch, dinner

Mutsugoro (££)
A small restaurant in the basement of a hotel that specialises in seafood and local dishes (including lotus root and horse-meat).
✉ Kumamoto Green Hotel, 12-11 Hanabatacho ☎ (096) 325 2222 🕐 Lunch, dinner

Senri (££)
Located in the Suizenji Koen Park, the Senri serves eel and river fish and also horse-meat dishes.
☎ (096) 384 1824 🕐 Lunch, dinner

Miyazaki

Kuretake (£/££)
Located in the basement of an office building, this restaurant serves excellent local dishes such as local

vegetables, noodles and
hiyajiru, which is hot rice
with cold fish soup.
📧 **Nikko Bldg, Tachibana-Dori**
☎ **(0985) 242 818** ⏰ **Lunch,
dinner**

Naha (Okinawa)
Restaurant Naha (££–£££)
Local-style cooking using
fresh local ingredients. In the
evening there is a floor show
of traditional Okinawan folk
dancing.
📧 **2-4-2 Tsuji** ☎ **(098) 868
2548** ⏰ **Dinner**

Ryotei Naha (££)
Local-style cooking, often
accompanied by an authentic
folk dance show.
📧 **2-2-11 Tsuji** ☎ **(098) 868
2548** ⏰ **Dinner**

Sam's by the Sea (££)
This chain is run by an
American ex-military family,
and combines Western and
Japanese cooking. Large
portions and good service
are the hallmarks.
📧 **Naha Shopping Centre, 2-4-
17 Nishi** ☎ **(098)862 6660**
⏰ **Lunch, dinner**

Nagasaki
Fukiro (£££)
Rather an atmospheric old
wooden building with
screens and traditional seating near the Suwa Shrine. It
sells a Nagasaki speciality
called *shippoku*, which is a
collection of small dishes all
served together.
📧 **146 Kami Nishiyama-machi**
☎ **(095) 822 0253** ⏰ **Dinner**

Hamakatsu (££)
A restaurant well known for
shippoku (▶ above) and for
other local dishes, which are
served in a modern setting.
There is an illustrated menu

and two floors, the cheaper
part is downstairs.
📧 **1-14 Kajiyamachi** ☎ **(095)
823 2316** ⏰ **Lunch, dinner**

Harbin Restaurant (£–££)
A bit of a curiosity – a
restaurant specialising in
good Russian and French
food. There is an old-
fashioned European
atmosphere and reasonable
prices, with a menu in
English.
📧 **2-27 Kozenmachi** ☎ **(0958)
237 443** ⏰ **Lunch, dinner**
🚉 **JR Nagasaki**

Matsukaze (£££)
A restaurant serving set
breakfasts and lunches,
and high-quality *kaiseki* in
the evening. Located in a
hotel and with an English
menu.
📧 **Nagasaki Prince Hotel 4F,
2-26 Takaramachi** ☎ **(0958)
211 111** ⏰ **Breakfast, lunch,
dinner** 🚋 **Takaramachi
Streetcar Station**

Shikai-ro (£–££)
A huge restaurant on four
floors, which is capable of
serving 1,500 customers at
any one time. Some 200
years ago *champon*, a
Chinese-inspired dish of
thick noodles, was invented
here.
📧 **4-5 Matsugae-machi**
☎ **(0958) 822 1296** ⏰ **Lunch,
dinner**

Yagura Sushi (£–££)
A specialist *sushi* restaurant
that provides breakfast,
lunch and dinner sets at
good prices. There is an
English menu.
📧 **3-4 Yorozuyamachi**
☎ **(0958) 221 813**
⏰ **Breakfast, lunch and dinner.
Closed Thu**

Seasonings and
Condiments
Japanese cuisine uses
surprisingly few
seasonings, relying instead
on the natural flavour,
freshness and appearance
of the ingredients. Apart
from soy sauce (*shoyu*),
the most common
flavourings are: *miso*
(fermented soy-bean
paste), *goma* (toasted and
crushed sesame seeds
mixed with salt), *mirin*
(sweet, fortified wine,
similar to sherry); ginger
root; *toga-rashi* (a blend of
several spices, including
pepper); and *wasabi* (hot
horse-radish mustard).

Hokkaido & Northern Honshu

Prices

Prices are per room per night. Note that in business hotels and some *ryokans* breakfast is not included.

£ = ¥4,000–12,000
££ = ¥12,000–27,000
£££ = ¥28,000 and above

Apart from international-style hotels, and the inns known as *ryokan*, there are also *minshuku*, which are family homes that take in paying guests, much like traditional B&Bs. They are generally cheaper than other accommodation and offer an insight into Japanese life.

Akan
Yamaura Hotel (££)
Small lakeside hotel in Akan Kohan Village with mostly traditional-style rooms.
✉ Akan Kohan, Akan 085
☎ (0154) 672 311

Akita
Kohama Ryokan (£–££)
A traditional *ryokan* in a modern building. Fresh local dishes are served. Convenient for Kakunodate.
✉ 6-19-6 Nakadori Akita
☎ (018) 832 5739

Hakodate
Pension Hakodatemura (£)
Well located in the Motomachi waterfront section and with views of Mount Hakodate, this modern inn has 17 rooms.
✉ 16-12 Suehirocho
☎ (0138) 228 105

Kakunodate
Hyakusuien Minshuku (£)
This centrally located inn is in a 19th-century warehouse, which also houses a small museum.
✉ 31 Shimonaka-machi
☎ (0187) 555 715

Ishikawa Ryokan (£–££)
Modern, comfortable family *ryokan* with good food.
✉ 32 Iwase-machi ☎ (0187) 542 030

Otaru
Otaru International Hotel (££)
Comfortable hotel with mostly western-style rooms and swimming pool.
✉ 3-9-1 Inaho, Otaru 047 ☎ (0134) 332 161

Sado-shima
Sado Seaside Hotel(£–££)
Close to the port of Ryotsu, this is a modern Japanese-style hotel with hot springs.
✉ 80 Sumiyoshi, Ryotsu City
☎ (0259) 277 211

Sapporo
Hotel Alpha Sapporo (£–££)
High-quality hotel in the shopping district and convenient for the lively nightlife area.
✉ Nishi 5-9-1, Minami 1 Chuo-ku, Sapporo 060 ☎ (011) 221 2333

Hotel New Otani Sapporo (££–£££)
Well-located good-quality hotel close to the station.
✉ 1-1 Nishi, Kita-2, Chuo-ku
☎ (011) 222 1111

Sendai
Dochuan Youth Hostel (£)
This is in a converted thatched farmhouse on the edge of the countryside.
✉ 31 Kitayashiki, Onoda, Taihaku-ku ☎ (022) 247 0511

Sendai Hotel (££)
Close to the station, a modern, well-established hotel with over 100 comfortable rooms.
✉ 1-10-25 Chuo, Sendai, Miyagi 980 ☎ (022) 225 5171

Japanese Inn Aisaki (£)
A traditional-style inn founded in 1868 in a convenient location.
✉ 5-6 Kitamemachi, Sendai, Miyagi 980 ☎ (022) 264 0700

Towada-Hachimantai
Kuounso
Modern *ryokan* in traditional style with open-air hot spring surrounded by the natural beauty of the park.
✉ Matsukawa-onsen, Matsuomura, Iwate-gun
☎ (019) 578 2818

Central Honshu

Hagi
Tomoe Ryokan (££)
Charming old inn serving excellent food and set in attractive gardens. Bathrooms are shared.
✉ 608 Hijiwara ☎ (0838) 220 150

Hiroshima
ANA Hotel (££–£££)
One of the best hotels in the city, with good, comfortable rooms. Only 10 minutes from the station and close to the Peace Park. Swimming pool, sauna, gym.
✉ 7-20 Naka-machi, Naka-ku, Hiroshima 730 ☎ (082) 263 5111

Kamikochi
Nishi-Itoya Sanso Inn (££)
Traditional wooden building located near the Kappabashi Bridge. Meals available. Advance reservations essential in the summer.
☎ (0263) 952 206

Kanazawa
Kanazawa Tokyu Hotel (££–£££)
Modern hotel in the centre of town (10 minutes from station) with comfortable rooms.
✉ 2-1-1 Korinbo ☎ (076) 231 2411

Murataya Ryokan (£–££)
Modern wooden building with rooms in traditional Japanese style. Both Western and Japanese breakfasts available. Central location.
✉ 1-5-2 Kata-machi, Kanazawa 920 ☎ (076) 263 0455

Matsumoto
Enjyoh Bekkan (£–££)
A mountain hot spring resort on the outskirts of town with great views of the Japan Alps. Access to the hot spring 24 hours. Traditional rooms.
✉ 110 Utsukushigahara-onsen, Satoysmbe-ku ☎ (0263) 337 233
🚇 Utsukushigahara-onsen

Nagano
Hotel Nagano Kokusai Kaikan (££)
Medium-sized, mostly Western-style hotel with good rooms and central location.
✉ 576 Minami Chitose, Agata-machi, Nagano ☎ (0262) 341 111

Nagano Royal (££)
Hotel with over 100 Western-style rooms within a minute's walk of the station.
✉ 1-28-3 Minami-Chitose ☎ (0262) 282 222

Nagoya
International Hotel Nagoya (£–££)
Long-established, popular hotel with a European feel. Western and Japanese restaurants available.
✉ 3-23-3 Nishiki, Naka-ku, Nagoya 450 ☎ (052) 961 3111

Ryokan Meiryn (£)
Centrally located in a modern building, this is a good-value inn with Japanese-style rooms (without private bathrooms).
✉ 2-4-21 Kamimaezu, Naka-ku, Nagoya 463 ☎ (052) 331 8686

Takayama
Kinnikan Ryokan (££–£££)
Excellent and very comfortable traditional *ryokan* in the heart of the old town.
✉ 48 Asahi-machi, Takayama 506 ☎ (0577) 323 131

Bed & Breakfast
In some *ryokan* breakfast will not be included and you will have the choice of Japanese- or Western-style. In old-fashioned *ryokan*, however, a Japanese breakfast (rice, fish and *miso* soup) will be included and served to you on a tray in your room after the maid has rolled away your *futon*.

Curfew
When staying in the smaller hotels in Japan, you may well be subject to a curfew (probably 11PM at the latest), even in major cities like Tokyo. Pleading for a key will cut no ice – if you don't make it back, then you will have to make alternative arrangements.

Temple Stays
An interesting way of experiencing Japanese life is to stay in a *shukubo*, or temple lodging. Accommodation will be simple (though reasonably priced) and you may be permitted to join in prayers and meditation. Ask at a tourist information centre.

Business Class
Among Western-style hotels the best value are the so called 'business hotels', which offer comfortable, characterless, no-frills rooms that are rather small but spotlessly clean and very reasonably priced.

Pension Anne Shirley (£)
A peaceful, small wooden inn on the edge of town, about 10 minutes by taxi from the station.
✉ 87 1297-1 Yamaguchi-cho ☎ (0577) 326 606

Takayama Green Hotel (££–£££)
A short way west of the station, this comfortable hotel has both Japanese- and Western-style rooms. Hot spring bath and tennis court.
✉ 2-180 Nishinoisshiki-cho, Takayama 506 ☎ (0577) 335 500

Tokyo
Akasaka Yoko Hotel
Well located for both Roppongi and Akasaka, this is a small business hotel that is competitively priced, although rooms are rather small.
✉ 6-14-12 Akasaka, Minato-ku ☎ (03) 3586 4050

Gajoen Kanko Hotel (££)
Dating back to the 1930s, this hotel has plenty of wood panelling and old prints, and is very good value, although a little way from the centre. French and Chinese restaurants.
✉ 1-8-1 Shimo-Meguro, Meguro-ku ☎ (03) 3491 0111

Hilltop (££–£££)
This old-fashioned hotel has very comfortable rooms and seven restaurants, the best of which, the Yamanue, serves *tempura*.
✉ 1-1 Surugadai, Kanda, Chiyoda-ku ☎ (03) 3293 2311

National Children's Castle (£–££)
A great hotel for families with children (➤ 110), with an indoor/outdoor playground and a clinic. Traditional rooms.
✉ 5-53-1 Jingumae, Shibuya-ku ☎ (03) 3797 5677

Park Hyatt (£££)
Occupying the upper floors of the Shinjuku Park Tower, this is probably the most sophisticated hotel in Japan and one with marvellous views to boot. The large rooms are decorated with rare woods and natural fibres.
✉ 3-7-1-2 Nishi-Shinjuku, Shinjuku0ku ☎ (03) 5322 1234

Ryokan Sawanoya (£–££)
Located just northwest of Ueno Park, this friendly inn offers excellent value. Western or Japanese breakfast available. All rooms have basins, some have baths, and there is also a public bath.
✉ 2-3-11 Yanaka, Taito-ku 110 ☎ (03) 3843 2345

Ryokan Shigetsu (££)
Well located in Asakusa for the temple, shops and metro station, this is a comfortable inn with Western- and Japanese-style rooms. Curfew at 11PM.
✉ 1-31-11 Asakusa, Taito-ku ☎ (03) 3843 2345

Tokyo International Youth Hostel (£)
Located on the 18th floor of the Central Plaza Building, this hotel is cheap, clean and now and accepts anybody. Rooms have two, four, or five bunk beds. Reservations vital. Curfew at 10:30PM.
✉ 1-1 Kagurakashi, Shinjuku-ku ☎ (03) 3235 1107

Western Honshu & Shikoku

Iseshima
Futamikan Ryokan (££–£££)
Old and traditional inn located on the coast with very good food and beautiful views.

 569-1 Futami-cho, Mie Prefecture 519 ☎ **(05964) 32003**

Kobe
Kobe Bay Sheraton (£££)
Located on Rokko Island, the Sheraton has the usual amenities associated with the chain, including sauna, tennis courts and swimming pool.

✉ **2-13 Koyocho-naka, Higashinada-ku** ☎ **(078) 857 7000**

Sannomiya Terminal (££)
Located over the railway station, the Sannomiya has comfortable Western-style rooms at reasonable prices.

✉ **8-1-2 Kumoidori, Chuoku** ☎ **(078) 291 1121**

Kochi
Kochi Dai-ichi Hotel (££)
Moderately priced hotel with Western-style rooms close to the station.

✉ **2-2-12 Kita-honmachi** ☎ **(088) 883 1441**

Kochi Green Hotel (£–££)
Simple but comfortable, this modest hotel is close to the station.

✉ **3-1-11 Harimaya-cho, Kochi** ☎ **(088) 822 1800**

Koyasan
Henjosonin Temple (£)
Pleasant rooms overlooking a garden, and good vegetarian food.

✉ **Reihokanmae** ☎ **(0736) 562 514**

Kyoto
Hotel Alpha
Business hotel with very good location, comfortable rooms and excellent Japanese restaurant.

✉ **Kawaramachi, Sanjo-agaru** ☎ **(075) 241 2000**

Kyoto Park Hotel (££)
Japanese- and Western-style hotel in the eastern part of town close to the National Museum, convenient for the Gion area.

✉ **Sanjusangendo Side** ☎ **(075) 525 3111**

Kyoto Royal (££)
Large hotel with Western-style rooms in excellent location in the central part of the city.

✉ **Sangoagaru, Kawaramachi, Nakakya-ku** ☎ **(075) 223 1234**

Ryokan Kyoka (£)
Good central location, a traditional inn at good prices. No private bathrooms. Western and Japanese breakfasts available.

✉ **Higashi-iru, Higashinotouin, Shimojuzuyamachi-dori** ☎ **(075) 371 2709** 🚇 **JR Kyoto Station**

Ryokan Murakamiya (£)
Wooden inn in central location close to the Higashi Honganji Temple. All the rooms are in traditional Japanese style. No private baths. Japanese breakfast.

✉ **270 Sasayacho, Shichijoagaru, Higashinotouin-dori, Shimogya-ku** ☎ **(075) 371 1260**

Tawaraya Ryokan (£££)
Expensive inn considered one of the finest in the country and for which reservations are essential.

✉ **Fuyacho, Oike-Sagaru, Nakagyo-ku** ☎ **(075) 211 5566**

For Your Convenience
Traditional Japanese toilets are uncomfortable to use at first, although ultimately healthier. Squat facing the cistern, the water from which can also be used for washing your hands.

Camping

The cheapest way of seeing Japan is camping but you may have to provide your own equipment. Furthermore, many camping sites are open only during the summer, which is also the period when they are invaded by students. A leaflet is available from JNTO.

Kurashiki
Ryokan Kurashiki (££)
In the heart of the old town, this inn has been constructed from warehouses and an old merchant's house. The adjoining restaurant is excellent.

✉ 1 Honmachi ☎ (086) 422 0730

Matsuyama
ANA Hotel Matsuyama (££–£££)
The best hotel in the city, well located for the castle and a 10-minute ride from the station. Mostly Western-style rooms.

✉ 3-2-1 Ichiban-cho ☎ (089) 933 5511

Taikei Business Hotel (££)
This cheerful establishment has more character than most business hotels. Public baths on the premises.

✉ 3-1-15 Heiwa Dori, Matsuyama 790 ☎ (089) 943 3560

Nara
Nara Fujita Hotel (£–££)
An hotel not far from the station with 115 Western-style rooms. Comfortable and reasonably priced.

✉ 47-1 Shimo-Sanjocho ☎ (0742) 238 111

Ryokan Seikan-so
With a charming Japanese garden and a central location, this inn offers good value. No private bathrooms. Japanese and Western breakfasts available.

✉ 29 Higashi-Kitsuji-cho ☎ (0742) 222 670

Osaka
Ebisu-so Ryokan (£)
Located in a shopping quarter not far from Namba and the National Theatro. Japanese-style rooms without private bathrooms.

✉ 1-7-33 Nipponbashi-nishi, Naniwaku, Osaka 556 ☎ (06) 643 4861

Holiday Inn Nankai (££)
Close to Namba Station, shopping and nightlife areas, with good, comfortable rooms and Western and Japanese restaurants.

✉ 2-5-15 Shinsaibashisuji, Chuo-ku, Osaka 542 ☎ (06) 213 8281

Hotel New Otani (£££)
One of the best and most expensive hotels in the city in an exotic modern building close to the castle. Sophisticated service and excellent gym.

✉ 1-4-1 Shiromi, Chuo-ku, Osaka 540 ☎ (06) 941 1111

New Naniwa Hotel (££)
Large *ryokan* with 25 Japanese-style rooms with their own bathrooms and 5 Western-style rooms. Breakfast and dinner available. Short walk from Nihombashi Station.

✉ 2-10-12 Shimanouchi, Chuo-ku ☎ (06) 213 1241

Takamatsu
Takamatsu Kokusai Hotel (££)
With mostly Western-style rooms, this is a comfortable hotel with swimming pool. About 10 minutes by car from the station.

✉ 2191-1 Kitacho ☎ (087) 831 1511

Tottori
Hotel New Otani Tottori (££–£££)
Very close to the station with comfortable, mostly Western-style rooms.

✉ 2-153 Imamachi ☎ (085) 723 1111

Tsuwano
Meigetsu Ryokan (££)
Very good *ryokan* in traditional style in the centre of the town.

✉ Tsuwano-cho, Kanoashi-gun 699-56 ☎ (0856) 720 685

Kyushu & the Southern Islands

Beppu

Suginoi Hotel (££–£££)

The largest and best-known hotel in the town, with self-contained facilities and huge baths.

 Kankaiji, Beppu 874
☎ (0977) 241 141

Fukuoka

Clio Court (££–£££)

Modern hotel with rooms decorated in different styles. Western and Japanese restaurants. Located immediately behind Hakata Station.

 5-3 Hakataeki-Chuogai, Hakata-ku 812 ☎ (092) 472 1111

Kagoshima

Nakazono Ryokan (£)

Centrally located, good-value inn. No rooms have private bathroom but there is a bath for common use and another that can be used privately.

☒ 1-18 Yasui-cho, Kagoshima 890 ☎ (099) 226 5125

Kumamoto

Kumamoto Castle Hotel (££)

Located close to the castle, and a 10-minute drive from the station, this comfortable hotel has mostly Western-style rooms.

☒ 4-2 Jotomachi, Joto-cho
☎ (096) 326 3311

Miyazaki

Miyazaki Plaza (££)

Riverside hotel with a number of Japanese-style as well as many Western-style rooms, all with bathrooms.

☒ 1-1 Kawara-machi
☎ (0985) 271 111

Mount Aso

Aso Kanko Hotel (££)

A small hotel with 30 Western-style rooms, hot-spring bath, tennis courts and swimming pool.

☒ Yunotani, Choyo-mura Aso-gun ☎ (09676) 70311

Aso National Park Flower Garden (£)

One of several inns in a 'pension' village with simple accommodation at very good inclusive (breakfast and dinner) rates.

☒ Takamori-machi, Ozu, Takamori 3096-4 ☎ (09676) 23012

Nagasaki

Hotel New Nagasaki (££–£££)

Located very close to the station, this modern, mostly Western-style hotel has a swimming pool and a gym.

☒ 14-5 Daikoku-machi, Nagasaki 850 ☎ (095) 826 8000

Minshuku Tanpopo (£)

Modern inn well located for the Peace Park with Japanese-style rooms and communal bath.

☒ 21-7 Hoeicho ☎ (095) 861 6230

Sakamoto-ya Ryokan (££)

Atmospheric traditional wooden inn about 10 minutes' walk from Nagasaki Station. Most rooms have their own bathrooms. Local specialities served.

☒ 2-13 Kanaya-machi
☎ (095) 826 8211

Naha (Okinawa)

Okinawa Harbour View (££–£££)

Located a short distance from the main street, this Western-style hotel has a swimming pool and sauna, and comfortable rooms.

☒ 2-46 Izumizaki, Naha-shi
☎ (098) 853 2111

Homestays

If you are interested in really experiencing Japanese life to the full, 'homestays' are possible. Information about this can be obtained from JNTO.

105

Antiques & Crafts

Souvenirs

Shopping in Japan can be an alarmingly expensive business but there will always be something colourful and intriguing to buy that is cheap – elaborate chopsticks, paper coasters, or wooden games and toys for example.

An unusual and cheap gift, if you can find it, would be *sake* in a can which heats itself automatically when the can is opened.

Antiques

Kyoto
Shinmonzen-dori
Long, narrow street filled with antique and art shops.
✉ Gion

Tokyo
Antique market
China, swords, woodblock prints and many other items.
✉ Hanae Mori Bldg, Omotesando-dori, 3-6-1 Kita-Aoyama ☎ (03) 3406 1021

Kurofune
Specialist for antique furniture, most of which has not been fully restored. Also sells prints and fabrics.
✉ 7-7-4 Roppongi

Mayuyama
Antiques emporium dealing in ceramics, screens and scrolls.
✉ 2-5-9 Kyobashi, Chuo-ku ☎ (03) 3561 5146

Tokyo Antique Hall
With over 30 stalls of curios and antiques, this is a good place to browse for bargains.
✉ 3-9-5 Minami-Ikebukuro ☎ (03) 3982 3433

Ceramics
Stoneware and porcelain are still produced in the traditional way throughout Japan. Different styles are associated with particular areas.

Imbe (Okayama)
Bizen Yaki Traditional Pottery Centre
✉ Imbe Station ☎ (086) 964 1001

Kyoto
Takashimaya Department Store
✉ Shijo-dori ☎ (075) 1221 8811

Kyushu
Arita Porcelain Park
🚌 Arita shuttle-bus from Arita Station

Mashiko (near Tokyo)
Hamada House
✉ Mashiko ☎ (0285) 723 223

Cloisonné

Tokyo
Ando
In business for over a century, this probably has the best choice in Japan.
✉ 5-6-2 Ginza ☎ (03) 3572 2261

Crafts

Kyoto
Kyoto Craft Centre
Plenty of exhibits and large choice of crafts for sale.
✉ 275 Gion, Kita-gawa, Higashiyama-ku, nr Maruyama-koen Park ☎ (075) 561 9660

Kyoto Handicraft Centre
Large selection of crafts.
✉ Kuimani Jinja Higashi, Sakyo-ku, nr Heian-jingu Shrine ☎ (075) 761 5080

Tokyo
Beniya Folkscraft Shop
Four floors of crafts from all over the country, and a coffee shop for recovery.
✉ 2-16-8 Shibuya ☎ (03) 3981 8437

International Arcade
Sells all types of Japanese crafts and souvenirs, including jewellery and kimonos.
✉ 1-7-23 Uchisaiwaicho, Chiyoda-ku ☎ (03) 3571 1528

Japan Sword
Best-known shop in Tokyo for traditional swords. Also deals in kitchen cutlery.
✉ **3-8-1 Toranomon** ☎ **(03) 3434 4321**

Kokkusai Kanko Kaikan
Tourism offices from Japan's various prefectures. Traditional wares from all over the country are sold. Ideal if you want to buy something from a particular area.
✉ **1-8-3 Marunouchi, Chiyoda-ku** ☎ **(03) 3215 1181**

Oriental Bazaar
Near the Hanae Mori building. Rummage through the extensive range of good-quality folding screens, pottery, fans etc.
✉ **5-9-13 Jingu-mae, Shibuya-ku** ☎ **(03) 3400 3933**
ⓒ **Closed Thu**

Tokyu-Hands
Famous store that reputedly has over 3 million different items for sale to meet all your DIY and hobby needs.
✉ **12-18 Udagawa-cho, Shibuya-ku**

Yamamoto Soroban Ten
Long-established family business specialising in abacuses, which are still widely used in Japan. Also sells instructions in English.
✉ **2-3-12 Asakusa** ☎ **(03) 3841 7503**

Dolls

Tokyo
Kyugetsu
One of the largest doll shops in the country, selling all types of traditional and modern Japanese porcelain and wooden dolls.
✉ **1-20-4 Yanagibashi, Taitoku** ☎ **(03) 3861 5511**

Yoshitoku
Long-established doll shop selling all kinds of Japanese dolls, including Kabuki figures, masks and fired-clay Hakata dolls.
✉ **1-9-14 Asakusabashi, Taito-Ku** ☎ **(03) 3863 4419**

Fans

Tokyo
Arai Bunsendo
In business for a century or more, this is one of the many colourful stalls close to the Kannon temple.
✉ **Nakamise-dori** ☎ **(03) 3844 9711**

Teaware

Tokyo
Tsutaya
A shop that specialises in everything you could possibly want for the traditional tea ceremony and also flower-arranging.
✉ **5-10-5 Minami Aoyama, Minato-ku** ☎ **(03) 3400 3815**

Woodblock Prints

Kyoto
Nishiharu
Excellent selection of woodblock prints with some explanations in English.
✉ **Teremachi Arcade** ☎ **(075) 211 2849**

Tokyo
Sakai Kokodo Gallery
The oldest woodblock print shop in the country, dating back to 1870. Originals and reproductions.
✉ **1-2-14 Yurakucho** ☎ **(03) 3591 4678**

Art Less
Don't be deterred from going into expensive art and antique shops. Many items might be impossibly expensive but there are bargains to be had, particularly in the art world – signed prints by eminent Japanese artists are often reasonably priced.

Modern Japan

Books & Music

Tokyo

Kinokuniya
This bookshop has a wide choice of books and magazines in English and a large number of useful items for foreigners studying Japanese.
✉ **3-17-7 Shinjuku (6th floor)** ☎ **(03) 3354 0131**

Kitazawa
Many books of all types on Japan, and also old and antique volumes.
✉ **2-5 Jimbocho** ☎ **(03) 3263 0011**

Tower Records & Books
International chain that apparently manages to sell magazines and books at lower prices than elsewhere in the city.
✉ **1-22-14 Jinan, Shibuya-ku** ☎ **(03) 3496 3661**

Virgin Megastore
Thousands of CDs and videos, and plenty of places for listening to your choices.
✉ **Marui 101 Bldg, 3-30-16 Shinjuku** ☎ **(03) 3353 0056**

Wave
A 'concept retailing outlet' with several floors of audio and visual software, CDs, sheet music and books.
✉ **6-2-21 Roppongi, Minato-ku** ☎ **(03) 3353 0056**

Department Stores

Tokyo

Matsuya
Good selection of folkcraft items, and very modern household goods, as well as kitchenware and clothing.
✉ **3-6-1 Ginza** ☎ **03 3567 1211**

Mitsukoshi
One of the oldest stores in Japan and still famous for its kimonos, as well as international designer labels.
✉ **1-4-1 Nihombashi Muromachi, Ginza** ☎ **(03) 3241 3311**

Printemps
A branch of the famous French store, which aims for a fairly youthful clientele. Announcements made in both French and Japanese.
✉ **3-2-1 Ginza** ☎ **(03) 3567 0077** 🌐 **Closed Wed**

Seibu
Modern, go-ahead store with excellent basement food hall and a specialist hardware section.
✉ **2-1 Udagawa Cho, Shibuya**

Takashimaya
This has become one of the best stores in the city with a vast array of designer goods sold in a floridly decorated setting.
✉ **2-4-1 Nihombashi, Chuo-Ku** ☎ **(03) 3211 4111**

Wako
Distinctive pre-war store on Ginza 4-chome Crossing which sells luxury international wares and specialises in Seiko watches.
✉ **4-5-11 Ginza** ☎ **(03) 3562 2111**

Electronics & Cameras

Osaka

Denden Town
General centre for electronic goods sales. Plenty of choice but try bargaining and check

that any item will work at home.

✉ **Nipponbashi**

Ninomaya

Five floors of tax-free electronic goods including hi-fi and watches.

✉ **4-11-2 Nipponbashi, Naniwaku** ☎ **(06) 643 2220**

Tokyo
Akihabara

The area of Tokyo famous for its array of electronic shops.

✉ **Akihabara**

Camera No Kimura

Sells a wide selection of used cameras. Open on Sundays.

✉ **1-18-8 Nishi Ikebukuro** ☎ **(03) 3981 8437**

Yodobashi Camera

Shinjuku is the photographic centre for Tokyo and Yodobashi is thought to be one of the largest camera shops in the world.

✉ **1-11-1 Nishi Shinjuku** ☎ **(03) 3346 1010**

Kimonos

Tokyo
Chicago

Sells used but often immaculate kimonos.

✉ **6-31-21 Jingumae** ☎ **(03) 3409 5017**

Mitsukoshi Department Store (▶ 108)

Paper

Kyoto
House of Kajinoha/Morita Washi

A small shop selling a tremendous array of handmade paper at good prices.

✉ **Kawaramachi** ☎ **(075) 341 1419**

Tokyo
Washikobo

A specialist in handmade paper and handicrafts.

✉ **1-8-10 Nishi Azabu, Minato-ku** ☎ **(03) 3405 1841**

Pearls

Ise Peninsula
Mikimoto Pearl Island

Tourist island entirely devoted to the production of pearls.

✉ **Toba**

Tokyo
Asahi Shoten

Wide selection of moderately priced pearls and pearl jewellery.

✉ **Imperial Hotel Arcade, 1-1-1 Wehisaiwaicho** ☎ **(03) 3503 2528**

Sake

Tokyo
Nihonsu Centre

Here you can sample five different kinds of *sake* for a fixed price. There is plenty of information about the drink and at the end you can keep the fifth *sake* cup.

✉ **5-9-1 Ginza** ☎ **(03) 3575 0654**

Toys

Tokyo
Hakuhinkan Toy Park

All sorts of toys including puzzles, games and jokes.

✉ **8-8-11 Ginza** ☎ **(03) 3571 8008**

Kiddyland

Very popular shop that specialises in jokes and tricks.

✉ **6-1-9 Jingu-mae** ☎ **(03) 3409 3431**

Warm Hands

The Japanese are adept at finding ways to cope with life's inconveniences. For children with frozen hands in the winter, you can buy *tsukaisute kairo*, packs which when rubbed become warm and can be kept in the pocket.

Children's Attractions

Safety

Japan is a safe country for children in terms of risk from child molesters, and Japanese children are allowed to walk about and travel on public transport by themselves from a very early age.

Fukuoka
Space World

The world's first space-orientated theme park. The large park includes large-scale rides, restaurants and a space camp. The space camp gives young people the opportunity to experience what it is like to travel in outer space.

✉ 8-1 Edamitsuhoncho, Yahata Higashi-ku, Kitakyushu-shi, Fukuoka-ken ☎ (093) 672 3600 💰 Moderate

Kobe
Kobe Municipal Suma Aqualife Park

Aquarium with trained dolphins that perform daily. Live indoor tanks and outdoor exhibits and rides make up the park.

✉ 1-3-5 Wakamiya-cho, Suma-ku, Kobe-shi, Hyogo-ken ☎ (078) 731 7301 🕐 Daily from 9–5, till 6 in summer. Closed Wed, except in summer 💰 Cheap

Kobe Portopialand

This amusement park on Port Island has plenty of rides and attractions for older children, but nothing much for children under six.

✉ 8-7-1 Minatojimanaka-machi, Chuo-ku, Kobe-shi, Hyogo-ken ☎ (078) 302 2820 🕐 Daily 10–5:30. Closed Wed (extended opening hours in summer) 💰 Moderate

Mount Fuji
Narusawa Ice Cave and Fugaku

Narusawa Ice Cave and Fugaku were both formed from a prehistoric eruption of Mount Fuji and are close to the road in the area around the smaller Lake Sai-ko. There is a bus stop at both caves or you can walk from one to the other in about 20 minutes.

Osaka
Banpaku Koen Expoland

This amusement park was built as part of Expo '70. Many rides and a playground for younger children.

✉ 1-1 Banpaku-koen, Senri, Suita-shi, Osaka-fu ☎ (06) 877 0560 🕐 Daily 9:30–5:30 (until 9 in summer). Closed Wed except in Aug 💰 Cheap

Osaka Aquarium

The aquarium has a variety of sharks and they and other fish share their quarters with the aquarium's star attractions, two enormous whale sharks. There are displays of life (including giant spider crabs) found on eight different ocean levels.

✉ 1-1-10 Kaigan-dori, Minato-ku, Osaka-shi, Osaka-fu ☎ (06) 576 5501 🕐 Daily 10–8. Closed Wed, Dec–Feb 💰 Moderate

Saitama
Saitama Children's Zoo

A 66-hectare park in a natural mountain setting.

✉ 554 Iwadono, Higashimatsuyama-shi, Saitama-ken ☎ (0493) 351 234 💰 Moderate

Tokyo
Korakuen Amusement Park

Traditional amusement park connected to Tokyo Dome Stadium, with rides to suit all ages.

✉ 1-3-61 Koraku, Bunkyo-ku, Tokyo ☎ (03) 3817 6098 🕐 Daily 10–7, until 9 in summer 💰 Cheap

National Children's Castle

More of an activity centre for

children than an amusement park, with play rooms, audio-visual rooms, swimming pool for children only, library, computer room and so on.

✉ 5-53-1 Jingu-mae, Shibuya-ku, Tokyo ☎ (03) 3797 5666 🕐 Weekdays 12:30–5:30, weekends 10–5:30. Closed Mon 💵 Cheap

Oume Railway Park (Oume Tetsudo No Koen)

Steam locomotives are on display and the trains run throughout the day. You can also play on locomotives in the park and view the miniature railway's panorama. The railway museum is about a 15-minute walk from Oume station.

✉ 2-155 Katsunuma, Oume-shi, Tokyo ☎ (0428) 224 678 🕐 Daily 9–4:30. Closed Mon 💵 Moderate

Sesame Place

Based on the Sesame Street TV series, the attractions are interactive, safe and very good for young children.

✉ 403 Ajiro, Itsukaichi-machi, Nishitama-gun, Tokyo ☎ (0425) 965 811 💵 Cheap

Tepco Electric Energy Museum

Seven floors with displays covering anything and everything associated with electricity.

✉ 1-12-10 Jinnan, Shibuya-ku, Tokyo ☎ (03) 3477 1191 🕐 Daily 10:30–6:30. Closed Wed 💵 Moderate

Tokyo Disneyland

Near perfect replica of its American original, with the Disney characters played by American actors and park signs in English. Shuttle buses run at 15-minute intervals from Tokyo Station, Ueno Station and Yokohama Station.

✉ 1-1 Maihama, Urayasu-shi, Chiba Prefecture, Tokyo ☎ (0473) 540 001 🕐 Daily, but times vary according to season 💵 Moderate

Tokyo Metropolitan Children's Museum (Tokyo-to Jido Kaikan)

The second floor features an athletics corner and slide show. The fourth floor is equipped for aspiring artists to make stained glass, pottery, painted flowers and nameplates. There is a library on the fifth floor.

✉ Shibuya ☎ (03) 3409 6361 💵 Moderate

Toshimaen

Oldest amusement park in Tokyo, with 50 attractions. Large adult rides, haunted houses and a special children's section.

✉ 3-25-1 Koyama, Nerima-ku, Tokyo ☎ (03) 3990 3131 💵 Cheap

Yokohama

Children's Land (Kodomo no Kuni)

A model farm, zoo, playgrounds, free cycling, children's rides, greenery and scattered woods, meadows and a lake.

✉ Tsurukawa Sta (Odakyu Line), by bus to Kodomo no Kuni ☎ (045) 961 2111 💵 Cheap

Hakkeijima Sea Paradise

Vast marine amusement park with modern aquarium, watersport attractions and thrilling rides such as the 'surf coaster' over the sea.

✉ Hakkeijima ☎ (045) 788 8888 🕐 Daily 9–9 💵 Moderate

Christmas

Although Christmas has no indigenous religious foundation in Japan, it is still celebrated. Father Christmas may not, however, leave the presents in the bedroom or under the tree, but, perhaps, outside.

The Arts

Body Art

The tradition of *irezumi* or tattooing has become an art form. Intricate designs covering the body were originally a way of branding criminals but nowadays they tend to be favoured by the Yakuza, commonly thought of as the Japanese mafia.

Kabuki Theatre

Kyoto
Minami-za Theatre, Kyoto
The oldest *kabuki* theatre in Japan. Main festival is 1–26 December.
✉ Shijo-Kamagawa, Gion
☎ (075) 561 1155

Osaka
Shin Kabuki-za
A modern *kabuki* theatre.
✉ 4-3-25, Namba, Chuo-ku, Osaka ☎ (06) 631 2121

Tokyo
Kabuki-za Theatre
The most famous *kabuki* theatre in the city.
✉ 4-12-15 Ginza ☎ (03) 3541 3131

National Theatre, Tokyo
Stages all types of theatre including *kabuki*.
✉ 4-1 Hayabusacho, Chiyoda-ku ☎ (03) 3265 7411

Noh & Kyogen Theatre

Kyoto
Kongo Nogaku-do
There are performances on the fourth Sunday of each month except August.
✉ Muro-machi Shijo
☎ (075) 221 3049

Kanze Nogaku-do Kaikan
Performances on the fourth Sunday of each month except July.
✉ 44 Enshoji-cho, Sakyo-ku, South of Heian Shrine
☎ (075) 771 6114

Osaka
Osaka Nogaku Kaikan
Regular performances of *noh* theatre.
✉ 2-3-17 Nakazaki-Nishi, Kita-ku. Just east of Osaka Station ☎ (06) 373 1726

Tokyo
Ginza Noh-gakudo
✉ Sotobori-dori, 5-15 Ginza 6-chome, Chuo-ku ☎ (03) 3571 0197

National Noh Theatre (Kokuritsu No-gakudo)
✉ 4-18-1 Sendagaya, Shibuya-ku ☎ (03) 3423 1331

Kanze Noh-Gakudo
Located in Shibuya.
✉ 1-16-4 Shoto ☎ (03) 3469 5241

Bunraku Puppet Theatre

Kyoto
Gion Corner
Stages various traditional performances including *bunraku*.
✉ Yasaka Hall, Hanamikoji-dori ☎ (075) 561 1119

Osaka
National Bunraku Theatre
The home of *bunraku* (► 70).
✉ 1-12-10 Nipponbashi, Chuo-ku, Nipponbashi
☎ (06) 221 2531

Tokyo
National Theatre
Stages all types of theatre. See entry under Kabuki.

Dance

Kyoto
Gion Kobu Kaburen-jo
The Miyako Odori (Cherry Blossom Dance) is performed four times a day throughout April by apprentice *geisha*.

☒ **Gion Corner** ☎ (075) 561 1115

Pontocho Kaburen-jo Theatre
Dances (Kamogawa Odori) similar to the Cherry Blossom Dance at Gion, are performed here 1–24 May and 15 Oct–7 Nov.
☒ **Sanjo-sagaru, Nakagyo-ku, Pontocho** ☎ (075) 221 2025

Osaka
Takarazuka Grand Theatre
Revues and kitsch female dance troupe.
☒ **Takarazuka** ☎ (06) 079 7840321

Tokyo
Tokyo Takarazuka Gekijo
Tokyo version of the famous Osaka revue.
☒ **1-1-3 Yurakucho** ☎ (03) 3591 1711

Drumming

Niigata (Northern Honshu)
Sado-ga-shima
Traditional *taiko* drum music played daily 1 Apr–3 Nov.

Classical Western Music
Check with venues or local tourist information centres for programme information.

Osaka
Ishihara Hall
☒ **1-3-15 Edobori, Nishi-ku, Higobashi** ☎ (06) 444 5875

Izumi Hall
☒ **Osaka-jo Koen** ☎ (06) 944 1188

The Symphony Hall
☒ **Close to Fukushima Station** ☎ (06) 453 6000

Tokyo
NHK Hall
☒ **2-2-1 Jinnan, Shibuya-ku** ☎ (03) 3465 1751

Suntory Hall
☒ **Ark Hills, 1-13-1 Akasaka** ☎ (03) 3505 1001

Rock/Jazz

Osaka
Large choice of bars and clubs in the area of Minami-ku, particularly around Shin-saibashi and Amerikamura.

Tokyo
Cavern Club
Features house bands performing *Beatles* music.
☒ **5-3-2 Roppongi** ☎ (03) 3405 5207

New York Bar
Most sophisticated jazz venue in Tokyo.
☒ **Park Hyatt Hotel** ☎ (03) 5322 1234

Shinjuku Pit Inn
Long-established club featuring Japanese and foreign musicians playing jazz fusion and blues.
☒ **3-16-4 Shinjuku** ☎ (03) 3354 2024

Film

Tokyo
Cinevivant
Specialises in European films, mostly new works.
☒ **Wave Building, 6-2-27 Roppongi** ☎ (03) 3403 6061

National Museum of Modern Art
Japanese classics and foreign films shown at weekends.
☒ **Kitanomaru Koen Park** ☎ (03) 3561 0823

Cinema
The 1950s are considered the golden age of Japanese film. In 1951 *Rashomon*, directed by Kurosawa Akira (➤ 14), won the main prize at the Venice Film Festival, and his *Shichinin-no-Samurai* (Seven Samurai) was the basis of Hollywood's *The Magnificent Seven*.

Sporting Activities

Watersports

People in Tokyo who crave water activities should make their way to the beautiful Kamakura area, where windsurfing, waterskiing and many other sports are popular.

Baseball

Tokyo & Environs

Chiba Lotte Marines
✉ Chiba Marine Stadium, 1 Mihama, Mihama-ku, Chiba City
☎ (043) 296 1189

Nippon Ham Fighters
✉ Tokyo Dome, 1-3-61 Koraku, Bunkyo-ku ☎ (03) 3811 2111

Seibu Lions
✉ Seibu Lions Stadium, 2135 Kami Yamaguchi, Tokorozawa City, Saitama Prefecture
☎ (0429) 251 151

Yakult Swallows
✉ Jingu Stadium, 13 Kasumigaokamachi, Shinjuku
☎ (03) 3404 8999

Yokohama Bay Stars
✉ Yokohama Stadium, Yokohama Park, Naka-ku, Yokohama City ☎ (045) 661 1251

Yomiuri Giants
✉ Tokyo Dome, 1-3-61 Koraku, Bunkyo-ku ☎ (03) 3811 2111

Cycling

In many towns renting a bike is the perfect way to explore. Cycle hire outlets are often near the main station. The main thing to be aware of, away from main tourist centres, is that street names are only given in Japanese script, so it can be hard to find exactly where you are. The English-language cycling newsletter *Oizake* (available from Brian Harrell, 2-24-3 Tomigaya, Shibuya-ku, Tokyo ☎ (03) 3485 0471) is packed with useful advice.

Hokkaido

Shibetsu-shi Cycling Terminal
18km park course and a longer alternative route to lake.
✉ 9-7 Higashi Shichijo-kita, Shibetsu ☎ (01652) 23822

Kyoto & Environs

Yasumoto Rental Bikes
✉ Kwabata Sanjo, Sakyo-Ku
☎ (075) 751 0595

Kyohan Rental Bikes
✉ Arashiyama, Ukyo-Ku
☎ (075) 861 1656

Rentopia Service
✉ Hachijo Exit, Kyoto Station
☎ (0875) 672 0662

Sago Rental Bikes
✉ Futagoaka Bridge, Maruta-Marutamachi, Ukyo-Ku

Osaka

Bicycle Information Centre
Sells parts and also holds exhibitions.
✉ Osaka-kyujo Bunka Kaikan, 2-8-110 Namba Naka ☎ (06) 643 5231

Kansai Cycle Sports Centre
The centre boasts a 3km circuit, dirt courses and bikes for hire.
✉ 1304 Amano-cho, Kawachinagano-shi ☎ (0721) 543 100

Tohuku

Morioka-Shi Tohan cycling terminal
37km lakeside cycling path and 24km path to Yahaba hot springs.
✉ 1-1-41 Yuzawa, Morioka-ohi, Iwate Ken ☎ 0196 370 876

Tokyo & Environs

Bicycle Culture Centre (Jitenshu Bunka Centre)
Shop, museum and anything to do with cycling.
✉ Jitensha Kaikan Bldg, 3, 1-

9-3 Akasaka, Minato-ku
☎ (03) 3584 4530

Cycle Sports Centre
Outside Tokyo. There are
bikes for hire and circuits to
follow.
✉ 1826 Ono, Shuzenji-cho,
Shizuoka ☎ (0558) 790 001

Japan Cycling Association
✉ Jitensha Kaikan Bldg, 3, 1-
9-3 Akasaka ☎ (03) 3583 5628

Wakayama
Kawabe-cho Cycling Terminal
✉ 2095 Wasa, Kawabe-cho,
Hidaka-gun, Wakayama-ken
☎ (0738) 530 234

Hiking

Mount Fuji (▶ 16)
The climb to the top can be
good fun though crowded
and strenuous, and is
achieved by nearly half a
million people of all ages
every year. The most
popular starting point is
Kawaguchiko Fifth Station.
✉ Fuji-Hakone-Izu National
Park ⏱ Jul & Aug only
🚌 Bus to Kawaguchiko
from Hamamatsucho or
Shinjuku

Horse Riding

Tokyo
Avalon Riding Club
✉ 3-19-2 Noge, Setagaya-ku
☎ (03) 3702 1770
🚉 Futakotamagawaen

Martial Arts

Aikido World Headquarters
☎ (03) 3203 9236

All-Japan Judo Federation
✉ Kodokan, 1-16-30 Kasuga,
Bunkyo-ku ☎ (03) 3818 4199

Japan Karate Federation
✉ Sempaku Shinkokai
Building, 1-15-16 Toranomon
☎ (03) 3503 6637

All-Japan Kendo Federation
✉ Nippon Budokan,
Kitanomaru Park, Tokyo
☎ (03) 3211 5804

Skating

Tokyo
Hibiya Ice Rink
This 19m by 30m outdoor
rink, modelled after New
York's Rockefeller Center
rink, is situated in the centre
of town. Lessons available.
✉ Hibiya Kokusai Bldg, 2-2-3
Uchisaiwaicho, Tokyo ☎ (03)
3595 0295 🚉 Uchisaiwaicho
👆 Cheap

Sumo Tournaments

Fukuoka
Nov (2nd Sun-4th Sun)
✉ Fukuoka Kokusai Centre
Sogo Hall, 2-2 Chikuko-
Honmachi, Hakata-ku ☎ (092)
272 1111

Tokyo
Jan and May (1st or 2nd
Sun–3rd or 4th Sun), Sep
(2nd Sun–4th Sun)
✉ Kokugikan Sumo Hall, 1-3-
28 Yokoami, Sumida-ku ☎ (03)
3623 5111

Nagoya
Jul (1st Sun–3rd Sun)
✉ Aichi-ken Taiikukan, 1-1
Ninomaru, Naka-ku ☎ (052)
9/1 2516

Osaka
Mar (2nd Sun–4th Sun)
✉ Osaka Furitsu Taiikukaikan,
3-4-36 Namba Naka, Naniwa-ku
☎ (06) 631 0120

Sumo
Sumo wrestlers tend to be
huge. Of course, this is
deliberate and is achieved
by eating foods like
chankonabe, a very fatty
stew and by using arcane
methods of expanding the
intestines.

What's On When

Cherry Blossom Viewing

Between March and May cherry blossom viewing (*hanami*) parties assemble all over Japan, the exact dates depending on the ripening blossom in the particular region. Local television stations give updates on the state of blossom ripeness in each area. The most popular place to see the blossom in Tokyo is Ueno Park, and in Kyoto, the gardens of the Heian Shrine.

January

New Year's Day (1 Jan): the most important holiday of the year, involving a lot of shrine visiting and traditional games.

Grass Fire (15 Jan): bonfires and fireworks in Nara Park to commemorate the amicable settlement of a border dispute a thousand years ago.

February

Snow Festival (5–11 or 6–12 Feb): ice and snow sculptures are displayed throughout Sapporo and elsewhere on Hokkaido.

March

Takayama Matsuri (14–15 Mar): dating back to the 15th century, this is noted for its procession of beautiful floats through Takayama.

Fire Festival (mid–late Mar): this takes place near Mount Aso and features fire torch swinging, grassfire and a torchlight *noh* performance.

April

Buddha's Birthday (8 Apr): in all temples an image of Buddha is displayed and sweet tea poured over it.

May

Grand Festival of Toshugu Shrine, Nikko (17–18 May): centuries-old festival features a parade (on the 18th) of 1,000 people dressed in armour, escorting three palanquins through the Nikko streets.

Sanja Matsuri (nearest Fri, Sat, Sun to the 18th): about 100 *mikoshi* (portable shrines) assemble at the Asakusa Shrine, Tokyo and then parade around the 'parish'.

June

Takigi Noh (1–2 Jun): performed after dark, by blazing torchlight, on an open-air stage at the Heian Shrine, Kyoto.

July

O-Bon Festival (13–15 Jul): nationwide Buddhist festival in honour of the dead, which is almost as important as New Year.

August

Peace Ceremony (6 Aug): a ceremony held at the Peace Park in Hiroshima.

Yamaga Toro (15–16 Aug): a parade in Yamaga City, Kumamoto, of dancing women wearing *yukata* and with lighted lanterns on their heads.

Daimonji (16 Aug): a spectacular bonfire at summit of Mount Nyoigadake, Kyoto.

September

Yabusame (16 Sep): traditional horseback archery display at Tsurugaoka Hachimangu Shrine, Kamakura.

October

Marimo Matsuri (8–10 Oct): Ainu festival with dances performed by Lake Akan in Hokkaido and Lake Yamanaka in Yamanashi.

Jidai Matsuri (22 Oct): commemorates the founding of Kyoto in 794. Procession of over 2,000 people dressed in costume. Takes place at the Heian Shrine, Kyoto.

December

Chichibu Yomatsuri (2–3 Dec): one of the grandest float festivals in Japan takes place at Chichibu in Saitama.

Practical Matters

Above: three monkeys 'hear no evil, see no evil, speak no evil' on Tokugawa Ieyasu's tomb, Nikko

Right: whistle seller at Hakone.

忠太郎

民芸品小鳥笛

TIME DIFFERENCES

GMT
12 noon

Japan
9PM

→ **Germany**
1PM

← **USA (NY)**
7AM

→ **Netherlands**
1PM

→ **Spain**
1PM

BEFORE YOU GO

WHAT YOU NEED

	UK	Germany	USA	Netherlands	Spain
● Required / ○ Suggested / ▲ Not required					
Passport/National ID card valid for 6 months from date of entry	●	●	●	●	●
Visa	▲	▲	▲	▲	▲
Onward or return ticket	▲	▲	▲	▲	▲
Health inoculation	▲	▲	▲	▲	▲
Health documentation (reciprocal agreement document)	●	●	▲	●	●
Travel insurance	●	●	●	●	●
Driving licence (international and national)	●	●	●	●	●
Car insurance certificate (hire car)	●	●	●	●	●
Car registration document (hire car)	●	●	●	●	●

WHEN TO GO

Tokyo

■■■■■ High season
▭▭▭▭▭ Low season

8°C	9°C	12°C	17°C	21°C	25°C	28°C	31°C	26°C	21°C	15°C	11°C
JAN	FEB	MAR	APR	MAY	JUN	JUL	AUG	SEP	OCT	NOV	DEC
☀	☀	☀	☀	☀	🌧	🌧	⛅	⛅	☀	☀	☀

🌧 Wet   ☀ Sun   ⛅ Sunshine & showers

TOURIST OFFICES

In the UK
Japan National Tourist
Organisation (JNTO)
Heathcoat House
20 Savile Row
London W1S 3PR
☎ (020) 7734 9638

In the USA
JNTO
One Rockefeller Plaza
Suite 1250
New York City
NY 10111
☎ (212) 757 5640

JNTO
360 Post St
Suite 601
San Francisco
CA 94108
☎ (415) 987 7140

POLICE 110
FIRE 119
AMBULANCE 119
Japan Helpline: (0120) 461 997
Other crisis lines – See local phone book

WHEN YOU ARE THERE

ARRIVING

Most visitors arrive by air, and unfortunately land at the large, impersonal Narita Airport and then have to make the tedious journey into Tokyo. The modern Kansai International Airport has been built on a huge man-made island in Osaka Bay to serve Kyoto, Osaka and Kobe. It operates 24 hours a day.

Narita (Tokyo) Airport
Distance to city centre

Journey times

66 kilometres

- 🚆 60–90 minutes
- 🚌 90–120 minutes
- 🚗 90–120 minutes

Kansai Airport
Connections to Osaka

Journey times

- 🚆 30–60 minutes
- 🚌 50–60 minutes
- 🚗 50–60 minutes

MONEY

The monetary unit of Japan is the Japanese yen. Coins come in ¥1, ¥5, ¥10, ¥50, ¥100, ¥500 denominations, and there are ¥1,000, ¥5,000 and ¥10,000 notes. Major credit cards are accepted in all large cities and most airports and city banks have facilities for changing foreign currency and travellers' cheques. Ouside large cities credit cards may not be accepted everywhere and cash is more dependable.

TIME

Japan is 9 hours ahead of Greenwhich Mean Time (GMT+9). The whole country lies within the same time zone. Daylight saving time is not used.

CUSTOMS

YES
There are specific allowances of alcohol, cigarettes and gifts that a person may bring into the country; alcohol and tobacco can only be brought in by those over 20 years of age.

Alcohol: 3 bottles (760cc each)
Tobacco products: 400 cigarettes or 100 cigars or 500g of tobacco
Perfume or toilet water: 57g/2fl oz
Gifts up to ¥200,000. There are no restrictions on currency importation, but not more than ¥5 million may be exported.

NO
Drugs, firearms, pornography (the average girlie magazine might not qualify for entry).

EMBASSIES AND CONSULATES

UK
Tokyo
(03) 3265 5511

Germany
Tokyo
(03) 3473 0151

USA
Tokyo
(03) 3224 5000

Netherlands
Tokyo
(03) 5401 0411

Spain
Tokyo
(03) 3583 8531

WHEN YOU ARE THERE

TOURIST OFFICES

The Japanese National Tourist Office (JNTO) operates the main tourist information centres listed below (except the one in Narita Airport). They advise on travel and accommodation and stock useful free literature. Most towns have their own tourist offices, often in the main JR (Japan Railways) station.

Kyoto
- 1st Floor
  Kyoto Tower Building
  Higashi-Shiokoji-cho
  Shimogyo-ku
  Kyoto 600
  ☎ (075) 371 5649

Osaka
- Passenger Terminal Building, 1st Floor
  Kansai International Airport
  Izumi-Sano
  Osaka 549
  ☎ (0724) 566 025

- Osaka Railway Station
  ☎ (06) 6345 2189

Tokyo
- B1F, Tokyo International Forum
  3-5-1 Marunouchi
  Chiyoda-ku
  Tokyo 100
  ☎ (03) 3201 3331

- Passenger Terminal 2, 1st Floor
  Tokyo Narita Airport
  Chiba 282
  ☎ (0476) 346 251

NATIONAL HOLIDAYS

J	F	M	A	M	J	J	A	S	O	N	D
2	1	2	1	2				2	1	2	1

1 Jan	New Year's Day
15 Jan	Adults' Day or Coming of Age Day
11 Feb	National Foundation Day
20 or 21 Mar	Vernal Equinox Day
29 Apr	Greenery Day
3 May	Constitution Memorial Day
5 May	Children's Day
15 Sep	Respect for the Aged Day
23 or 24 Sep	Autumn Equinox Day
10 Oct	Health and Sports Day
3 Nov	Culture Day
23 Nov	Labour Thanksgiving Day
23 Dec	Emperor's Birthday

In addition there are a large number of local and religious festivals – consult the nearest tourist information office.

OPENING HOURS

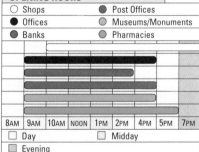

○ Shops   ● Post Offices
● Offices   ○ Museums/Monuments
● Banks   ○ Pharmacies

8AM	9AM	10AM	NOON	1PM	2PM	4PM	5PM	7PM

☐ Day   ☐ Midday
☐ Evening

Many shops stay open until 10PM. Some, in particular department stores, are open on Sundays and may instead close on a weekday (a different day for each store in a town).
Banks generally shut at noon on Saturday.
Museums often close slightly earlier during the winter months and are closed all together over the New Year holiday. They are usually also shut one day a week; if a national holiday falls on the museum's weekly closing day, it closes on the following day instead.

**DRIVE ON THE
LEFT**

**TOILETS
FREE**

PUBLIC TRANSPORT

 Internal Flights There is a comprehensive domestic air network. Flights are not always more expensive than Shinkansen (bullet train) and are faster for the longer journeys. There are five major carriers to choose from, and some discount fares are available – ask the airline for conditions.

 Trains Rail is the main means of transportation in Japan, and is fast and efficient. The system is a privatised network that operates under the JR (Japan Railways) banner, and includes various local services and the famous long-distance bullet trains (Shinkansen). The fare structure is complicated and planning is recommended. Anyone intending to travel around Japan should purchase a Japan Rail Pass, only obtainable outside Japan (see your nearest JNTO). JR Infoline (Tokyo): ☎ (03) 3423 0111.

 Coach Travel Travelling by coach on the comprehensive national network of JTB long-distance routes is much cheaper than travelling by Shinkansen, but is also much slower. If, however, time is not an issue but money is, then bus travel is worth considering – the overnight buses have reclining seats and are very comfortable.

 Ferries There are ferry services linking all the islands to one another. In economy class you will probably share one large *tatami* mat room with everyone else. Private cabins are also available.

 Urban Transport Many major cities have metro systems and in some cases, notably Tokyo, this is the best way (sometimes combined with city 'overground' or 'mass-transit' systems) of getting around. In other cases, notably Kyoto, the metro is of limited help and it is far better to rely on the excellent city bus service, where you pay as you alight.

CAR RENTAL

 Car rental is possible and may be recommended in a limited way – exploring a local rural area, for example. Otherwise it is more trouble than it is worth. Traffic congestion is a problem, and off major roads, signs are only given in Kanji (Chinese script).

TAXIS

 Taxis should be used sparingly – perhaps for the initial journey in a strange town – as they are terrifyingly expensive. They operate on a meter and drivers are honest. You should be prepared with your destination written down in Japanese.

DRIVING

 Speed limit on highways: **80kph**

 Speed limit on all country roads: **50–60kph**

 Speed limit on urban roads: **40–50kph**

 It is compulsory for drivers and passengers to wear seat belts at all times.

 Random breath testing is widespread. Drinking and driving is severely punished.

 Fuel is available as leaded and unleaded petrol and as diesel, and is sold by the litre. It is usually served by exceptionally helpful attendants. Credit cards are not always accepted.

 If driving a rental car, you should contact the car rental company, which will arrange to send road service to your location and repair the vehicle. Alternatively, most petrol stations will be able to assist or, at least, direct you to the nearest repair centre. Check with your own motoring club regarding reciprocal facilities.

PERSONAL SAFETY

One of the joys of Japan is that it is extremely safe. Theft is not out of the question, however, and although it is a rarity you are advised not to be complacent and to take the usual precautions. Japan is in a busy earthquake zone and all hotels display instructions on what to do should one occur.

Police assistance:
☎ **110**

TELEPHONES

Public telephones are ubiquitous and reliable, and colour-coded according to the calls you can make from them. Local calls (costing ¥10) can be made from pink, red or blue phones, and long-distance calls from yellow or green ones, but not IDD. Payphones accept both cash and phonecards (which can often be bought from a machine attached to the phone or from many shops). The major telephone company is KDD, but there are now also two competitors – IJT and IDC. International calls from public phones can be made using a KDD Super World Card, available from major shop chains like

Lawson, Familymart and 7-Eleven. For the international operator dial 0051.

International Dialling Codes

From Japan dial 001 (KDD), 0041 (ITJ) or 0061 (IDC) then:

UK:	44
Germany:	49
USA & Canada:	1
Netherlands:	31
Spain:	34

POST

Post offices are open 9–5 Mon–Fri and on Sat 9–12:30. The airmail rate for postcards is ¥70. Letters should be weighed to establish the rate. Write addresses clearly to help the Japanese sorters.

ELECTRICITY

The power supply is 100 volts AC, but Tokyo and eastern Japan are on 50Hz, while western Japan operates on 60Hz. American electric equipment that operates at 110/60 should work fine, but Europeans will need to adjust 240/50 devices. Sockets accept flat two-pin plugs, as in the US.

TIPS/GRATUITIES

Yes ✓ No ✗		
Restaurants (a service charge may be included)	✗	
Bar Service	✗	
Taxis	✗	
Tour guides	✗	
Hairdressers	✗	
Chambermaids	✗	
Porters (hotel)	✗	
Theatre/cinema attendants	✗	
Toilets	✗	

What to photograph: mountains, gardens, temples, modern urban Japan and glimpses of living 'old' Japan (eg *geisha* girls).
When to photograph: the best times are in the spring (especially when the blossom is out) and in the autumn.
Where to buy film: although it may be cheaper outside Japan, film of all types and processing facilities are widely available in even the smallest Japanese town.

HEALTH

Doctors
Medical insurance is essential as treatment is very expensive, though excellent. The following clinics have English-speaking doctors: Hibiya Clinic, Hibiya Mitsui Bldg, 1-1-2 Yurakucho Chiyoda-ku, Tokyo (☎ (03) 3502 2681); Japan Baptist Hospital, 14 Yamanomotocho Kitashirakawa, Kyoto, Sakyo-ku (☎ (075) 781 5191).

Dental Services
Dental services are good and widespread, but expensive. In major cities English-speaking dentists are not hard to find.

Sun advice
The Japanese summers are hot and sticky – it is easy to become dehydrated so it is essential to drink plenty of water or tea.

Drugs
Bring a good supply of prescription drugs in case they are difficult to find. Japanese pharmacies sell much the same range of everyday medicines you would find in Western Europe or America. There is an English-speaking chemist at the American Pharmacy in the Hibiya Park Building in Tokyo (☎ (03) 3271 4034).

Safe Water
Tap water is safe throughout Japan. Mineral water is also widely available. Beware of drinking from mountain streams as there is a risk of contracting tapeworm, and don't paddle barefoot in rice paddies or in stagnant water.

CONCESSIONS

Students/Youths
Discounts of up to 35 per cent are available on internal flights on JAL, ANA and JAS for those under 21. To register take a passport, passport photograph, and fee to an airline office.

Senior Citizens
Discounts are available for those over 65 on internal flights of JAL, ANA and JAS – proof of age will be required. There is also a discount available for train travel, but the JR Pass, available only outside Japan, is far better value.

CLOTHING SIZES

Japan	UK	Europe	USA	
36	36	46	36	
38	38	48	38	
40	40	50	40	Suits
42	42	52	42	
44	44	54	44	
46	46	56	46	
7	8	41	8	
7.5	8.5	42	8.5	
8.5	9.5	43	9.5	Shoes
9.5	10.5	44	10.5	
10.5	11.5	45	11.5	
11	12	46	12	
14	14	36	14.5	
15	15	38	15	
15.5	15.5	39/40	15.5	Shirts
16	16	41	16	
16.5	16.5	42	16.5	
17	17	43	17	
8	6	34	6	
10	8	36	8	
12	10	38	10	Dresses
14	12	40	12	
16	14	42	14	
18	15	44	16	
4.5	6	38	6	
5	6.5	38	6.5	
5.5	7	39	7	Shoes
6	7.5	39	7.5	
6.5	8	40	8	
7	8.5	41	8.5	

WHEN DEPARTING

- There is an airport tax payable on leaving Japan.
- Make sure that you reconfirm your onward flight no fewer than 72 hours before departure, especially if flying on a Japanese airline.
- Arrive at the correct airport with plenty of time to spare. If travelling to Narita Airport by bus, catch one at least 3 hours before departure time.

LANGUAGE

On the whole few Japanese people speak much English, although those that do are often willing to try it out on you. Knowledge of a few words and phrases is therefore likely to be useful. Pronunciation is straight forward, similar to Spanish or Italian. Pronounce each word exactly as it is written and you should be understood. There is no tone system as in Chinese; give each syllable equal stress. When addressing people, always use the surname, not first name, plus the suffix -san (for Mr, Mrs or Ms), but never add -san to your own name.

hotel	*hoteru*	for bed and breakfast	*choshokutsuki*
room	*rumu*		
single/double/ twin (room)	*shinguru/daburu/ tsuin (rumu)*	toilet	*o-tearai*
Japanese-style room	*washitsu*	Japanese-style bath	*o-furo*
Western-style room	*yoshitsu*	(Western) bed	*beddo*
		does that include…?	*wa tsuite imasu-ka?*

bank	*ginko*	two	*ni*
post office	*yubin-kyoku*	three	*san*
postage stamp	*kitte*	four	*yon/shi*
seal or stamp	*hanko*	five	*go*
how much is this?	*kore wa ikura desuka?*	ten	*ju*
credit card	*krejitto-kahdo*	twenty	*niju*
one	*ichi*	hundred	*hyaku*
		thousand	*sen*

restaurant	*resutoran*	boxed lunch	*bento*
pub/bar	*izakaya*	the bill	*kanjo*
cafe	*kissaten*	water	*mizu*
set menu	*teishoku*	beer	*biru*
lunch	*tanchi/hiru gohan*	just a little, please	*sukoshi*
dinner	*yushoku/ban gohan*	this is good	*oishi desu*
		knife and fork	*naifu to hawk*

aeroplane	*hikoki*	station	*eki*
airport	*kuko*	platform	*homu*
bus	*basu*	does this train/bus go to…?	*kono kisha/basu wa … e ikimasu-ka?*
bus stop	*basu tei*		
railway	*stationeki*	straight ahead	*masugu*
one day open ticket	*furii-kippu*	right	*migi*
single/return	*katamichi/ofuku*	left	*hidari*

yes	*hai*	I don't speak Japanese	*nihongo wa dekimasen*
no (rarely used)	*iio*		
please	*o-negai shimasu*	my name is…	*watashi wa…desu*
thank you	*domo arigato*		
no, thank you	*ii-desu*	what is this called?	*kore wa nanto iimasuka*
good morning	*ohayo gozaimasu*		
	konnichi-wa	help me!	*tasukete!*
good afternoon	*sayonara*	what time?	*nanji?*
goodbye	*gomen nasai*	excuse me!	*sumimasen!*
sorry	*how much?*	*ikuru?*	

INDEX

Acknowledgements
The Automobile Assocation wishes to thank the following photographers, libraries and associations for their assistance in the preparation of this book:

MARY EVANS PICTURE LIBRARY 2; ROBERT HARDING PICTURE LIBRARY 57c; JAPAN NATIONAL TOURIST ORGANISATION 9c; MRI BANKERS' GUIDE TO FOREIGN CURRENCY 119; NATURE PHOTOGRAPHERS LTD 12b (S C Bisserot); REX FEATURES LTD 14b; SPECTRUM COLOUR LIBRARY 5b, 16b, 31b, 42b, 71a, 75a; WERNER FORMAN ARCHIVE 11b (Kuroda Collection, Japan)

The remaining photographs are held in the Association's own photo library (AA PHOTO LIBRARY) and were taken by Jim Holmes, with the exception of the following: F/cover (e) Great Buddha, B/cover, 9d, 17b, 17c, 20b, 22b, 23b, 24b, 25b, 27a, 41, 42a, 47, 52a, 52b, 64b, 66b, 66c, 67c, 74, 122a, which were taken by Douglas Corrance

Copy editor: Caroline Dandy   Revision Management: Pam Stagg